THEY LIKE TO NEVER QUIT PRAISIN' GOD

THEY LIKE TO
NEVER QUIT
PRAISIN' GOD

*The
Role of
Celebration
in Preaching*

FRANK A. THOMAS

Foreword by Henry H. Mitchell

THE
PILGRIM
PRESS
Cleveland

The Pilgrim Press, Cleveland, Ohio 44115
© 1997 by Frank A. Thomas

Printed in the United States of America on acid-free paper

06 05   7

Library of Congress Cataloging-in-Publication Data

Thomas, Frank A. (Frank Anthony), 1955–
    They like to never quit praisin' God : the role of celebration in preaching / Frank A. Thomas ; foreword by Henry H. Mitchell.
        p.   cm.
    Includes bibliographical references.
    ISBN 0–8298–1181–8 (pbk. : alk. paper)
    1. Afro-American preaching.   2. Afro-American public worship.   3. Afro-Americans—Religion.   I. Title.
    BV4208.U6T43 1997
    251 ′.0089 ′96073—dc21   97–212
                                                            CIP

To my wife, Joyce,
for 20 years of marriage,
for 19 years of ministry,
for 15 years of pastoring,
which adds up to 500 years of patience and love,
I say thank you!

Contents

Foreword

It is with understandable pride and deep satisfaction that I offer this foreword to Frank Thomas's landmark work on sermonic celebration, *They Like to Never Quit Praisin' God: The Role of Celebration in Preaching.* This is a topic of consuming interest to me, and it is central to any serious consideration of the African American pulpit tradition. One of the chief motivations of my own writing, research, and teaching has been to stimulate further writing and research that would establish a recognized corpus of analytical works with which to preserve, refine, and teach the best of the African American preaching tradition. Frank Thomas and his work are the firstfruits of the fulfillment of my cherished dream.

Apart from any personal interest of mine, however, are the topics of black celebration and preaching as a whole, which must be considered on their own merits. Preaching is without question one of the major elements of African American culture. It ranks with the spirituals and the blues, about which a great deal of both descriptive and analytical material has been written. But, notwithstanding its great importance in the culture, very little serious history or description of black preaching has been written. I first wrote such a book, *Black Preaching,* in 1970, but I know of no other book on the subject since, except for my own revisions (1990). My book *Celebration and Experience in Preaching* deals with serious analysis of black homiletical method, but it was alone in the field until Frank Thomas wrote the present work. This book, then, is of inestimable importance apart from anything I might feel as Thomas's teacher and friend.

Starting where I left off, this work carried the topic of celebration well beyond. The author has come up with crucial insights and needed terminology with which to further the scholarly discussion and increase the understanding needed in the classroom. Subtleties once left of necessity to intuitive absorption were in danger of being lost in the stream of cultural flux. The vagaries of preaching apprenticeships not rooted in standard, culturewide terms and concepts were threatening the survival of the art. Even the term *celebration* was not as widely used or understood as was essential to the very preservation of the tradition. Frank Thomas has contributed much to the meeting of this need, probing celebration to new depths.

In addition, for all cultures and homiletical traditions, he has related his findings to recent developments in homiletical theory generally and even to other disciplines as well. This helps greatly to strengthen homiletics in its position in theological academia. Too many seminaries have assigned homiletical instruction to faculty of other disciplines, on the assumption that anybody can teach a student how to preach. This book adds to the corpus of serious scholarship available to instructors for the purposes of achieving a more powerful pulpit, in an era of urgent need in the field.

This work is especially enriching to the wider corpus of homiletical thought, in that its grasp of folk phenomena is so fresh and well integrated into the whole. It is from sources like these that both music and literature are often expanded. Such an approach is needed in homiletics, to liberate the craft/discipline/art of preaching from its traditionally overcognitive captivity. There are, of course, many other facets of homiletics to be explored, but this is certainly an impressive contribution and model for future research and writing on the new/old approaches available for the preaching of the gospel.

HENRY H. MITCHELL
Atlanta, Georgia

Preface

I have experienced in the pew, in the pulpit, in the world, and
most of all in myself, a hunger for high-quality, effective preaching. In response to this hunger, I became a student and critic of
preaching. I wanted to know what good preaching was, and what
method of sermon construction and delivery was used to produce
good preaching. What was it that the best preachers did that those
of us who are not considered the best preachers did not do? Was
preaching more a matter of innate gift for the task than a method
that could be learned? Or could high-quality, effective preaching
be achieved with and by method? If so, which method and whose
method? As a preacher of African American heritage, I wondered
what peculiar gifts were/are the legacy of this preaching tradition
that could shed light on the subject of good preaching. With all of
these questions, I began the critical and earnest pursuit of my
fundamental concern: what is good preaching, and what method
can be employed to arrive at good preaching?

   After a time of preaching experience and study, I became convinced of the beauty, simplicity, art, depth, and faithfulness to the
biblical text of celebrative preaching. Upon close inspection, I
noticed that celebration transcended racial, ethnic, and cultural
backgrounds, denominational distinctions, and gender classifica-
tions. I noticed that any preaching that was good had strong elements of celebration. I arrived at the conclusion that celebration
was not only the genius of the African American preaching tradition, but an important component of any good preaching. I be-

came motivated to explore the role, theology, dynamics, method, preparation process, and guidelines of celebrative preaching.

The following pages reflect my learnings as a teacher and practitioner of preaching, but, more important, my reflections as a permanent student of preaching. I have discovered that this question of good preaching keeps one endlessly a student, and perpetually humble.

Acknowledgments

Thanks to the family of the New Faith Baptist Church of Matteson, Illinois, who have allowed me to experiment with preaching as their pastor for fifteen years.

Thanks to Henry Mitchell, Edward Wheeler, and Jeremiah A. Wright Jr., who planted the seed of celebration in me, and then watered it into growth.

Thanks to my colleagues known as the Mitchell-Wheeler Fellows at the United Theological Seminary, who kept telling me that I was on to something.

Thanks to my preaching students, who inspired me with the zeal they brought to the preaching class, especially the students at McCormick Theological Seminary and the Thomas-Welbourne Fellows.

Thanks to Donnette Vaughn and Cynthia Forn for reading and rereading the manuscript and offering encouragement when I almost quit.

Thanks to Carolyn Ann Knight for road testing the manuscript in so many of her homiletics classes and believing that one day it would be published.

Thanks to Kim Sadler, my gifted editor, who challenged me to believe in the preaching insights that were within me.

Thanks to Larry Welbourne, friend, mentor, confidant, and prayer partner.

Thanks to my mom, dad, sister, and brother—it really does begin and end at home with you all.

Thanks to Tony and Rachel, who gave generously of family time for Dad to be on the computer. Not one word would have been written without your love.

1

Celebrative Design and
Emotional Process

The field of study known as homiletics, or the art of preaching, has been heretofore primarily dominated by Western thought and procedure. If we look at who has written and published, who has set forth homiletical method as taught in formal, academic settings, it has been traditionally the classical European and Euro-American male preacher.[1] But let us be careful to understand that other cultures and genders have homiletic methods. The best of the African American preaching tradition, for example, has clearly demonstrated homiletic genius, but it has been passed on in the folk culture, in the oral tradition, not set forth in published works and taught in academic institutions.

One brief example of the genius of the oral African American homiletic tradition is an account of a sermon entitled "Uncle Wash's Funeral,"[2] found in slave narratives compiled in 1936. Ned Walker, a layperson, heard the sermon somewhere around 1866–67 and, because it evidenced elements of true homiletic genius, he could vividly remember the experience almost seventy years later:

> Now 'bout Uncle Wash's funeral. You know Uncle Wash was the blacksmith in the fork of the road, across the railroad from Concord church. He had been a mighty powerful man. He used the hammer and the tongs on behalf of all the people for miles and miles around.
>
> Uncle Wash joined the Springvale A.M.E. Church, but he kinda fell from grace, I guess. Somehow he was 'cused of stealing Marse Walter Brice's pig, and I guess he was guilty.

At any rate, he was convicted and sent to the penitentiary. While he was down there, he contracted consumption and had to come home. His chest was all sunk in, and his ribs was full of rheumatism. He soon went to bed and died. . . .

Uncle Pompey preached the funeral . . . and Uncle Pompey really knowed how to preach a funeral. . . . Uncle Pompey took his text from that place in the Bible where Paul and Silas was a-layin' up in jail. He dwelt on Uncle Wash's life of hard work and bravery—how he tackled kickin' horses and mules, so's crops could be cultivated and harvested and hauled. He talked 'bout how he sharpened dull plow points to make the corn and the cotton grow, to feed the hungry and clothe the naked. He told what a good-hearted man Uncle Wash was, and then he 'llowed as how his goin' to jail did not necessarily mean he didn't go to heaven. He declared it wasn't eternally against a church member to get put in jail. If it hadda been, Paul and Silas wouldn't a made it to heaven, and he knowed they was there. In fact, they was lot a people in heaven what had been arrested.

Then he went to talkin' 'bout a vision of Jacob's ladder. "I see Jacob's ladder. An' I see Brother Wash. He's climbin' Jacob's ladder. Look like he's half way up. I want y'all to pray with me that he enter the pearly gates, Brothers and Sisters. He's still a climbin'. I see the pearly gates. They is swingin' open. An' I see Brother Wash. He has done reached the topmost round of de ladder. Let us sing with all our hearts that blessed hymn, "There Is a Fountain Filled with Blood."

When they sang the second verse, 'bout the dyin' thief rejoiced to see that fountain in his day, Uncle Pompey cried out over the crowd, "I see Brother Wash as he enters in, an' that dyin' thief is there to welcome him in. Thank God! Thank God! He's made it into Paradise. His sins has been washed away, an' he has landed safe forever more."

Well sir, I don't need to tell you that the women started to shout on the first verse, an' when they got to singing' 'bout the dying thief in heaven, *an' they seen the 'surance of grace that was in it, they like to never quit praisin' God.*

Usually, when confronted with the preaching tradition of African American preachers, people take great notice of the emotional intensity, energy, and freedom of the preacher and the people in the sermon and worship event. In Walker's story this emotional freedom appears in the phrase "the women started to shout." But for the purposes of this work, I would like to concentrate on another phrase in the story—"the 'surance of grace." When the people experienced the assurance of grace in the sermonic event, Walker says, "They like to never quit praisin' God." A closer look at this " 'surance of grace" is the center of our focus.

When Walker interprets the assurance of grace as the source of the praise of God, he puts his finger on the pulse and heartbeat of the best of the African American preaching tradition. Fundamentally, African American preaching is about helping people experience the assurance of grace that is the gospel. Let me state this as a formal definition:

> The nature and purpose of African American preaching is to help people *experience the assurance of grace* (the good news) that is the gospel of Jesus the Christ.

It is this assurance of grace, received through African American preaching and worship that has historically sustained, encouraged, and liberated African American people.

The story of "Uncle Wash's Funeral" illustrates the traditional role of the African American preacher. In the midst of profound anguish and suffering, the African American preacher sought not to give answers to the problem of suffering and evil in life, but to help people experience the assurance of grace in God. The preacher gave assurance to the people that God was with them, in and through the suffering, and would ultimately liberate them from the suffering. The point was not abstract answers to suffering and evil, but an experience of assurance, hope, empowerment, and victory. The focus was not on cognitive explanations, but an experience of the transforming, sustaining, and saving power of God in the midst of suffering and evil. The African American sermon was designed to celebrate, to help people *experience the assurance of grace* that is the gospel. For purposes of this work, I would like to name this preaching tradition celebrative design.[3]

Following the thought of Henry H. Mitchell,[4] I have long believed that the genius of African American preaching has been its ability to celebrate the gospel. The concept of celebration will be fully developed later, but suffice it to say that celebration is the natural response when one has received and appropriated the assurance of grace of the gospel. In Ned Walker's story, when the preacher helped people experience the assurance of grace, Walker says, "They like to never quit praisin' God."

CELEBRATIVE DESIGN AND EMOTIONAL PROCESS

In order to facilitate the experience of the assurance of grace, celebrative design gives strict attention to emotional context and process. To make clearer what is meant by emotional context and process, we must briefly consult the thinking of Edwin H. Friedman. Friedman believes society views communication as an exclusively cerebral process. Society typically assumes that when one wants to communicate, one engages in a cerebral process that takes ideas, wraps them in words and symbols, and transmits them to another person. The other person decodes the message according to similar cerebral processes, and comprehends the message. This can occur only in the most neutral of environments, however, and because anxiety is the static in any communication system, there are few neutral environments. Human communication is rarely free from anxiety, and therefore attention must be given to the emotional context in which communication takes place. Friedman articulates the thinking of celebrative design when he makes this assertion:

> Both theater and therapy [and preaching] share a common impulse—an attempt to go beyond the everyday forms of communication to shift people's basic notions of themselves and their world. Both represent a revolt against the normal use of discourse, an understanding of the natural limits of rhetoric and a recognition that *communication is at least as much an emotional phenomenon as a linguistic one.*[5]

Friedman's use of the term *emotional* does not mean paying attention to feelings typically known as emotions but to the emotional
context in which the communication takes place. This context is
established primarily by the relationship of the people who are trying to communicate, or could be conceptualized as the "emotional
field" that comes into existence when they attempt to relate.[6] Because most relationships are governed by this emotional field, paying
attention to the emotional context is more important than the choice
of the right words. Because communication is rarely neutral, there
are natural limits to what words can accomplish. Friedman says:

> Most of the world's religions, for all their emphasis on holy
> writ, and sacred teaching of the masters, have understood the
> limitations of words. From the very beginning, it was realized
> that even holy words were not necessarily efficacious. In fact,
> drama first emerged out of a desire to add spectacle and inten-
> sity to religious observance.[7]

It is precisely because so much of Western preaching has ignored
emotional context and process, and focused on cerebral process and
words, that homileticians most recently have struggled for new methods to effectively communicate the gospel.

After a period of great transition and flux, Euro-American homiletics today has exploded into many pieces, and is not close to set-
tling down. This explosion centers around the reality that the deductive rationalistic methodology, heavily influenced by Greek logic and
rhetoric, has broken down. Because the focus was primarily on words,
the old method sought from the scriptural text a proposition or idea;
a sermon was then written to elaborate deductively from this proposition, and persuade the listener. The sermon was rationalistic in approach and orientation, with little attention to emotional process.
The goal of the sermon was to demonstrate truth, illustrate truth,
logically deduce truth, and lead people to intellectually assent to truth.
This by nature required an analytical, objective style that sought to
impart information or give instruction. This style required people to
be generally passive in the process, waiting for the minister to convince them of the truth of the proposition. This analytical style was

far removed from the experience and folk traditions of average everyday people, who intuitively understand the operation and result of emotional process.

The result of this focus on the intellect was that many churchgoers found sermons boring, nonproductive, not worthy of interest or attention. In what sounded like a great crescendo, Western homileticians expressed the concern that people were not "hearing" the gospel. In other words, people were not responding to the preached word; the gospel seemed to have no impact upon the everyday life of the listener. Homileticians observed that the old method, humorously characterized as "three points and a poem," could not get the gospel heard or practiced today.

Homileticians began to ask several critical questions that would move the field in new directions: How can we get the gospel to be relevant to people's lives? How can we assist people to "experience" truth rather than just intellectualize it? How can we involve the listener in the sermonic process? How can we get the gospel to appeal beyond the rational aspects of ourselves? How can we get the gospel heard in depth, and made effective in the practical everyday life of the listener?

As homileticians continue to grapple with these questions, there has been a renewed concern for emotional context and process. Homileticians have discovered that whenever emotional context is diminished, or ignored, the communication process falters. The best of the African American preaching tradition, as in "Uncle Wash's Funeral," excels at giving attention to emotional context and process.

The preaching ministry of the French pastor André Trocmé is an excellent example of a non–African American preacher giving masterful attention to emotional context and process. Though Trocmé was most noted for leading his congregation to shelter five thousand Jewish refugees during World War II, listen to what was said of his preaching ministry:

> He is a pulpit orator who is absolutely original, who surpasses in authority anyone I have ever heard speak from the "chaire." He begins in a simple, familiar mood, starting with recent events, everyday or religious, then he raises himself, little by little, analyzes

his own feeling and thought, confesses his own heart with a sincerity and a [clarity] which disturb one; he uses the popular language, and sometimes crude language. . . . Is he not going to fall into trivialities? . . . But no! See him raising himself up . . . he climbs, climbs always higher . . . he draws us to the peaks of religious thought . . . and once we are at the summit, he makes us hover in a true ecstasy; then gently . . . he descends slowly to earth and gathers you in a feeling of peace which gives the last word "Amen" all the meaning the word has etymologically. One sits there afterwards . . . eyes clouded with tears, as if one has been listening to music that has seized you by your [inner parts].[8]

This is the kind of effect preaching can have when the preacher, regardless of race, ethnicity, gender, or cultural background masterfully attends to emotional context and process.

FIVE ELEMENTS OF EMOTIONAL PROCESS

If a preacher wants to focus on the emotional context rather than the choice of the right words, what will the preacher attend to? If the preacher wants to move beyond the natural limits of cerebral process, what elements of emotional process can be incorporated in the sermon? Five key elements will be explained and discussed in the following sections.

Use of Dialogical Language

The preacher who is concerned about emotional process must use language that fosters dialogue between the preacher and the people. Wellford F. Hobbie helps us discover characteristics of language that fosters dialogue when he credits Amos N. Wilder, in his book *Early Christian Rhetoric: The Language of the Gospel*,[9] with identifying the major modes of dialogical discourse in the Gospels: narrative, parable, and poetry. Characteristics of these modes that make the forms dialogical are:

proximity to oral conversation, in that language is immediate, spontaneous, and not discursive in style; the speech is related to the everyday concrete life of the community of faith; and the speech places the listener into the scene to evoke from him or her some response.[10]

As we look closely at "Uncle Wash's Funeral," we find all three of these characteristics clear and evident. The language of the sermon was not discursive or academic, but immediate, spontaneous, in the style of oral conversation ("You know Uncle Wash was the black-smith in the fork of the road, across the railroad from Concord church"). The speech was from the concrete everyday life and experience of the listener ("How he tackled kickin' horses and mules, so's crops can be cultivated and harvested"). The listener was placed in the scene to evoke a response ("I see Brother Wash as he enters in [heaven], an' that dyin' thief is there to welcome him in"). Much will be said later of these characteristics, but the language of the preacher is concrete, rooted in the experience of the listener, and evokes a response by appealing to the senses.

The effect of the dialogical language of celebrative design is that it involves the listeners as partners in the preaching process. The language engages the people in the sermon, inviting them to be a part of and invest in the sermon. When people become a part of and invest in the sermon, they move more easily at the level of emotional process and experience the gospel more deeply and profoundly. In the classical rationalistic deductive method, it was as if the minister had come down from Mt. Sinai with a message from God, while the people waited passively for the revelation. But when dialogical language is used effectively, the people and the minister go up to the mountain of God *together* and encounter the word of God. If we are concerned about emotional process, we must use language that includes people.

Appeal to Core Belief

If the preacher would utilize emotional context and process in the preaching event, then the sermon must appeal to core belief. I believe human awareness involves three aspects of self: the cognitive, the emotive, and the intuitive. The cognitive is the faculty for reason and rational thought. The emotive is the base for the arousal of feelings and affections. The intuitive is the capacity for direct knowing or learning beyond the conscious use of reasoning. Contained within the intuitive is the collection of core belief, broad principles for living shaped by cognitive, emotive, and intuitive evaluation of life and experience. Emotional process and context involve the cognitive, emotive, and intuitive as equal partners in reaching core belief in the preaching process.

Faith, for example, does not reside in the cognitive, or the emotive, but in the intuitive aspects of human personality. Faith is born in a "reasonable encounter,"[11] within an emotive context, then moves to reside as a principle in the intuitive, informing core belief. If we preach to influence the cognitive, or the emotive alone, we miss the core belief system. This means we miss powerful principles and assumptions that shape the opinion and behavior of the hearer. Mitchell visualizes these intuitive principles and responses as "tapes" that record life and experience:

> Our intuitive responses to various experiences are like tapes played deep down in consciousness. If in early life we formed a habit of believing that the planet was safe, and God was caring for us, that amounts to a tape. In a crisis, we tend to "play" it again and live by that same habit of trust. If a child was mistreated or poorly cared for, that child will have emotional habits or tapes of fear and distrust.[12]

It is possible to preach and explain to people at the cognitive level that God is worthy of faith and trust, and miss altogether the childhood tape of fear and distrust that is "running" in the inner consciousness of the listener. When this happens, people intellectually assent with the preacher that God is trustworthy, but seriously struggle to trust God because the tape of distrust has not been addressed. The very same could be said of preaching to the emotive level in people. People will feel that God is trustworthy for the moment, but without a reasonable encounter to match the emotion, trust is not established as a principle in the intuitive, and the childhood tape of fear and distrust is never challenged.

Therefore, the role of preaching is to attempt to over-record the tapes of fear, hatred, prejudice, unforgiveness, anxiety, etc., and strengthen the tapes of hope, trust, love, forgiveness, etc., by reaching the core belief with the gospel. The term *over-record* does not mean repression, or any form of denial of pain, suffering, and evil. It means that within the emotional field of the sermon that brings an assurance of grace, people can honestly face the tapes of fear, hatred, and prejudice. It means that with the help of the Holy Spirit, people can make the choice to over-record these damaging and destructive tapes with trust and hope. Within the emotional field of the sermon that truly celebrates is the Spirit-led possibility that hope, joy, love, and trust will be strengthened in the inner core of the listener. If the preacher desires this kind of growth in the listener, then the sermon must appeal to core belief through treatment of emotional context and celebrative emotional process.

Concern for Emotive Movement

The third element of emotional process in the sermon is the concern for *emotive movement*. When the exclusive focus is on cerebral process, traditionally the preacher is distrustful of the direct intention to arouse emotion and move people. Celebrative design does not move people as an end in itself but rather as part of the emotional process whereby the message of the sermon shifts into the intuitive core belief of the hearer. Without emotive movement it is very difficult for the sermon to make the shift to intuitive principle in core belief.

Homileticians have always been concerned with movement, or continuity, in the sermonic design. H. Grady Davis describes the sermon design as an "audible movement [of thought] in time."[13] But for the vast majority of Western homiletics, movement of thought was primarily cognitive, and therefore not specifically designed to move people. The sermon was an argument of a proposition, and the concern was logical coherence to ensure the preacher could convince the people of the proposition. The sermon was concerned primarily with cognitive movement in deductive flow, with little appeal to emotive movement.

One way to discuss emotive movement is to do so by analogy to movement in a well-crafted piece of music. Each movement in a piece of music expresses a certain nuance or shade of meaning that registers in the emotive. Each movement builds upon the emotive effect of the previous movement, heightening and enhancing the melody that has already been created, until at the close of the piece, one is left with a clear meaning or experience that registers in the intuitive. Movement is experienced at the level of emotion in the emotive, but the total experience forms a message that registers in the intuitive. Music does not ignore the cognitive to secure emotive movement, but includes it as part of the process because it is not possible to move anyone without musical cognitive logic, i.e., measures, beats, scales, harmonics, etc. The very best in the field of music clearly do not stop at the level of the cognitive, or the emotive, but intend to move the listener as part of the emotional process to register meaning in the intuitive.

The tradition of celebrative design intends, as part of the emotional process of the sermon, emotive movement similar to musical movement. The sermon is a series of ideas and images (moves)[14] expressed in bundles of language that generate a certain nuance or shade of meaning that registers in the emotive. Each move builds upon the emotive effect of the previous move, heightening and enhancing what has already been created, until at the close of the sermon, one is left with a clear meaning or experience that registers in the intuitive. The sermon does not ignore the cognitive to secure emotive movement, but includes it as part of the process, because it is not possible to move anyone without the cognitive logic of the sermon, i.e., exegetics, theology, words, and rules of communication that inform rational discourse. Celebrative design does not intend to move people for the sake of moving people; rather it intends to move people as part of the process of impacting core belief.

Unity of Form and Substance

The preacher who would attend to emotional process in the sermon must be concerned with unity of form and substance. Substance is content, the sum total of the truth to be delivered to the people. Form is rhetorical strategy, the means of persuading people of the truth, or the shape the sermon will take to most effectively communicate the content. We must give attention not only to what we want to say (cerebral process) but also to how to say it so that it has the best chance of getting heard (rhetorical strategy). But when we give appropriate attention to emotional process, form and substance merge into one and make for powerful communicative expression.

Western homiletical thought, based on cerebral process, has been overly concerned with content. It has believed that what made a good sermon was sound biblical exegesis and theological reflection (words). Once the content was shaped, it was assumed that rational discourse was the best form in which to share the gospel. Celebrative design, based upon attention to emotional process, has discovered that rational discourse is only one of many forms in which to share the gospel, and usually not the most effective. Celebrative design is open to the many and varied forms that are needed to get the gospel heard and lived, such as narrative and character sketch.[15]

The homiletical insight of celebrative design is backed by the recent work of biblical scholars in the fields of literary and form criticism giving more attention to the balance of form and substance. Scholars are discovering that form is critically important to substance, and substance is critically important to form. Hobbie states, speaking of literary and form criticism:

> These studies pose the question whether form can be viewed only as a vehicle for content, to be discarded when the idea or concept or teaching has been extracted, or whether form and function are inseparable. They raise the question whether the preacher may be discarding on his or her study desk a basic element of interpretation.[16]

Along with Hobbie, H. Grady Davis speaks profoundly and insightfully about the connection between form and substance. When the preacher merges form and substance, the message has the element of "the right thing said rightly," or what Davis calls finality:

> Once the right thing is said rightly, there is a feeling of finality about it, as if it could never be said so well in any way but this. Thought does not have the feeling of finality until it is said rightly.[17]

Davis uses as an example the first line of John Keats's poem "Endymion," first expressed as "A thing of beauty is a constant joy."

Keats's roommate remarked that the line lacked something. After a time of pondering, Keats changed it to "A thing of beauty is a joy forever." This version has the element of finality, the sense that the idea could never be expressed so well in any way but this. The wise preacher gives careful attention to the joining of form and substance, such that by sheer force, the message will register in the intuitive, and it might be said that "the preacher said the right thing rightly."

Creative Use of Reversals

Any preacher who would attend to emotional process must give careful thought to paradox, paradoxical intention,[18] or—the term we prefer—reversals. Reversals are fundamental to human life and human communication. The greatest asset of the human mind very well could be its ability to experience paradox. If we look at the history of the human order, the most worthy pursuits and accomplishments have come as resolution to some paradox. Fantasy, play, humor, love, symbolism, faith, hope, religious experience, and creativity in both arts and sciences appear to be essentially paradoxical. I would even argue that reversal is the very basis of creativity itself.

There is something fundamental to fresh experience in human communication that is bound up with reversals. Reversals set the stage for fresh encounter, and communication that does not attend to reversals leaves unexplored the connections between emotional process, the creative process, and fresh encounter. *I have a sense of wonder about reversals, because I suspect that the preacher's ability to offer an assurance of grace is grounded in the ability of the preacher to deal with reversals and paradox.*

These are large claims and assertions, so let us clearly define reversals. Richard H. Armstrong suggests that a reversal is a deliberate disappointment within a relationship.[19] For Armstrong, the primary criteria for reversals are contained in two explicit assumptions about the nature of human beings. Humans beings have (1) a basic need for identity and authenticity, and (2) a basic need to move into relationship with others. In the attempt to develop our identity and authenticity, we deliberately engage in disappointing behaviors, that is, behaviors that are in distinct contrast to the projected expectations of others. The ability to choose disappointing behaviors, and to mean them, is the hallmark of personhood, selfhood, and identity. But even as we intentionally fail to meet the projected expectations of others, we have a need to move into relationship with others. The need for identity coupled with the need for relationship places us in paradox as we negotiate relationship with others.

When two people who are in paradox attempt to relate, the ability to communicate is primarily dependent on the relationship (the emotional context) between the two. This relationship is conceptualized as an emotional field that comes into existence as they relate. Reversal takes place within the emotional context, or emotional field, of the relationship. Armstrong conceptualizes the emotional field as a shared surface of two overlapping bubbles:

> [Relationships] can for purposes of exposition be compared to the shared surface of two overlapping bubbles. The two [overlapping bubbles] form a common surface that is not a simple continuum of the curvature of either one of them but a surface with properties all its own. . . . Reversals, then, I believe occur at this interface and must by definition occur without rupture of the shared surface.[20]

Reversals, then, are deliberate and disappointing behaviors in direct contrast to the projected expectations of others that do not rupture the shared surface, the emotional field of the relationship. Within the emotional field is contained the paradox of disappointing behavior and yet sustained relationship. Though we automatically and intuitively assume that relationship means nondisappointing behavior, the paradox of disappointing behavior and sustained relationship facilitates fresh encounter. Glenn N. Scarboro speaks of what occurs in this shared surface when he says of reversals:

The process of the reversal, as part of an active relationship between two people, seems to call into question the commitment to old ideas and offers a fresh sense of wonder about old patterns. Hence, the rigidity in orientation changes and other possibilities are experienced.[21]

At the place of the shared surface of the relationship, in the face of disappointing behavior and sustained relationship, one experiences a fresh sense of wonder about old patterns, behaviors, and beliefs. Reversals set the stage for fresh encounter.

It would probably be helpful at this point to give several examples of reversals. Many consider Murray Bowen[22] to have been extremely proficient at reversals. Friedman recounts a story that illustrates what we have been saying about reversals:

> Shortly after Bowen joined the Georgetown Medical School faculty, a story circulated . . . of a woman who had come to him for a pass to go home. According to the tale, she also asked for a prescription for sleeping pills, and as Bowen was writing out the prescription, she added that when she got home she was going to use them to kill herself. As the story was told, Bowen just went on writing the prescription, and without even looking up, asked, "Well, just how many do you think you'll need?" In one version, she went home, took them out, immediately became nauseated, and flushed them down the toilet.[23]

This, of course, is not to suggest that anyone uncritically try this technique if confronted with such a situation, but it does demonstrate that at the level of emotional context there are ways to deliver messages that affect people at core belief. This kind of affect has to do with the reversal of content through focus on emotional process. To deal with the content in the situation described above would have been to anxiously engage in a discussion of whether or not she should kill herself, which was part of her projected hope and expectation. The reversal was to disappoint her by being nonanxious about her plan in the context of sustained relationship. The lack of anxiety called into question her projected hopes and expectations, which are based on a commitment to old ideas, patterns, beliefs, and principles in core belief. Reversals set the stage for fresh encounter.

Jesus was a master at reversals and used them to teach the true meaning of mercy in one of the most beautiful and healing passages of the New Testament, the story in John 8:1–11 of the woman who had been caught in adultery. In order to trap Jesus, the scribes and the Pharisees brought the woman to Jesus. Making her stand before the group, they asked Jesus to agree with the position of the law that a woman caught in adultery should be stoned to death. Jesus bent down and began to write on the ground and, executing a reversal, said, "Let anyone among you who is without sin be the first to throw a stone at her" (v. 7). They came to accuse her and trap him, but his reversal placed them in intimate contact with their own sin. He disappointed them by being nonanxious about their plan, and in the midst of sustained relationship, focused them on their need for mercy and grace. His reversal so impacted their core belief that they experienced a fresh sense of wonder about the old ideas and patterns about the law, mercy, and justice. The result of the reversal was that they dropped their stones, accusation, and plan of entrapment, and left.

The writer of the Gospel assumed that Jesus was without sin and could cast a stone. Yet, Jesus executes another reversal with the woman caught in adultery at the level of emotional process, and continues to teach mercy. The text says in verse 10:

> Jesus straightened up and asked her, "Woman, where are they? Has no one condemned you?" She said, "No one, sir." And Jesus said, "Neither do I condemn you. Go your way, and from now on do not sin again."

As one without sin, Jesus could have thrown a stone. She expected that he would stone her, but deliberately executing a disappointing behavior in the midst of sustained relationship, Jesus said, "Neither do I condemn you." His reversal helped her experience a fresh sense of wonder about old patterns, behaviors, and beliefs about the law, mercy, and justice. His reversal of her projected expectations helped her experience a fresh encounter with divine mercy and grace in core belief. Now that she had been challenged at the level of emotional process in core belief, he moved to the level of cerebral process and said, "Go your way, and from now on, do not sin again." Now that she experienced reversal, and a fresh sense of wonder about divine grace, he could give a cognitive command. Jesus deals with cerebral process only after fresh encounter at the level of emotional process.

The very last example of reversal will be taken from the story recounted earlier in this chapter, "Uncle Wash's Funeral." Uncle Wash was accused of stealing a pig, went to jail for it, contracted consumption, and died. Uncle Pompey preached the funeral and moved at the level of emotional process to execute a reversal in the midst of the sermon. Ned Walker says:

He [Uncle Pompey] told what a good-hearted man Uncle Wash was, and then he 'llowed as how his goin' to jail did not necessarily mean he didn't go to heaven. He declared it wasn't eternally against a church member to get put in jail. If it hadda been, Paul and Silas wouldn't a made it to heaven, and he knowed they was there. In fact, they was lot a people in heaven what had been arrested.[24]

The projected expectation of the emotional field was that thieves were not permitted in heaven, and that a person who went to jail could not get to heaven. But the preacher executed the deliberately disappointing behavior of proclaiming that there were several people in heaven that had been to jail, among them such notable biblical personalities as Paul and Silas. The reversal allowed the hearers to have a fresh encounter with divine grace and mercy operating in Uncle Wash's life.

The preacher (Uncle Pompey) does not stop with the one disappointing behavior of proclaiming that several thieves went to heaven, but, as we shall discuss in detail later, builds upon the reversal to celebrate the sermon. Uncle Pompey announced the familiar hymn, "There Is a Fountain Filled with Blood," and the hearers understood that what makes it possible for thieves to get to heaven is that God executed the disappointing behavior of dying for sinners. Then, Uncle Pompey had them encounter the dying thief on the cross in the second verse of the song, and on the top rung of Jacob's ladder in heaven to welcome Uncle Wash in. The welcoming dying thief was visible and tangible evidence of God's disappointing behavior, and as such, allowed for a fresh encounter with divine mercy and grace. The hearers experientially understood that the same divine grace available for Paul, Silas, and the dying thief was available to Uncle Wash, and available to them as well. This series of reversals so raises the intensity of fresh encounter that the chronicler could only say of several hearers, "They like to never quit praisin' God."

The reader will undoubtedly ask how one facilitates the reversal as a vehicle for fresh encounter. It has much to do with flexible distance that allows one to be emotionally objective. We shall say much more about emotional objectivity in chapter 3, but emotional objectivity lowers anxiety in the emotional field, which, in turn, allows one to be open to play, creativity, paradox, and reversal. Reversals occur in an emotional climate that is calm, and relatively free of tension and anxiety. I notice that if I am calm, which means the anxiety is low in me, then reversals bubble into my awareness. Within the interaction, I find many entrées and avenues to humor, wit, play, creativity, and reversal. I may choose not to execute any, but they are available to be fashioned into a presentable form as impact upon the emotional field.

The best of celebrative design excels at giving attention to emotional context by incorporating these five elements of emotional process: use of dialogical language, appeal to core belief, concern for emotive movement, unity of form and substance, and creative use of reversals. Celebrative emotional process manages these five elements to generate creative and powerful sermonic forms to help people experience the assurance of grace that is at the heart of the gospel. The following chapters of this book will set forth the theology, dynamics, method, preparation process, and guidelines of celebrative preaching.

2

A Theology of Celebrative Preaching

In chapter 1, we suggested that the nature and purpose of African American preaching is to help people experience the assurance of grace (the good news) that is the gospel of Jesus Christ. Whenever the assurance of grace of the gospel is received and appropriated, the natural response is one of celebration and praise to God. This chapter looks closely at the assurance of grace (the good news) that begets celebration by examining its biblical and theological base. What is the good news of the gospel of Jesus Christ? How does God choose to spread this good news to the world?

JESUS: THE GOOD NEWS

The early New Testament community understood Jesus Christ himself to be the good news, and therefore its primary bearer. The Greek word for good news, or gospel, is *evangelion*. Originally, it signified the reward that was given to one who brought good news, but in later times it came to mean the good news itself, or the good message. *The New Testament good news is that in the life, death, and resurrection of Jesus the Christ, the dominion of God met and conquered the dominion of Satan, whereupon salvation was made available to all.* The Greek word for salvation, *soteria,* means deliverance, preservation, or being brought into safety. If we accept, through faith, the victory established by the *soterion* (savior), then we are delivered, preserved, made safe from the dominion of death. The good news is that God through Jesus Christ has forever defeated Satan, evil, and death in all of its forms and manifestations.

The theology and teaching of the early church affirmed Jesus as the good news, but what did Jesus understand the good news to be?

When Jesus preached the good news, what did he understand himself to be doing? What did Jesus perceive as his mission, role, and purpose? Let us closely examine the beginning of the ministry of Jesus to discern his understanding of the good news.

The writers of the Gospels of Matthew and Luke do not begin with Jesus fully grown and engaged in ministry. These writers give some sense of Jesus' preparation for ministry.[1] The very *least* that can be said is that Jesus had a unique relationship with the Holy Spirit from birth. The Holy Spirit was involved in the conception process, and walked closely with Jesus as he grew up in the household of Mary and Joseph and in the Jewish community of faith. But after thirty years of preparation and nurture, through the power of the Holy Spirit, Jesus sensed it was time to begin. He went down to the River Jordan and was baptized by John. The Holy Spirit descended upon Jesus, and sanctioned the time of beginning. The Spirit brought Jesus out of the water, and led him into the wilderness to fast and pray for forty days. In the deserted place, Satan came to tempt him, and in the temptations the nature of his ministry was clarified—his mission, his purpose, and also his opposition.

After the forty days, the temptations were ended, and in the power of the Spirit, Jesus came to his hometown, the community of faith that had nurtured him. He went into the synagogue, and the attendant gave him the scroll of the prophet Isaiah, implying that he read. He read Isaiah 61:1–2, stopped in the middle, rolled up the scroll, and began to teach, saying, "Today this scripture has been fulfilled in your hearing" (Luke 4:21).

It is significant that at the point of beginning his ministry, Jesus went to his home congregation to, shall we say, preach his first sermon. It is as if he is announcing himself, engaging in a rite of passage by declaring the work of his life. In this moment of profound clarity, he says in Luke 4:18ff:

> The Spirit of the Lord is upon me, for God has anointed me to bring good news to the poor. God has sent me to proclaim release to the captives and recovery of sight to the blind, to let the oppressed go free, to proclaim the year of the Lord's favor.

What he said in these few words spoke volumes of truth to those who were assembled. Jesus was quoting Isaiah 61, and though there is not time or space to deal with the tremendous complexity of the Book of Isaiah, we must look at it briefly to give ourselves the full impact of Jesus choosing this text to announce himself.

The message of Isaiah as declared by God's covenant and prophets was initially one of judgment, due to the sinful reliance of the people upon foreign powers outside the will of God. The people were carried off into slavery because they forsook the covenant (chapters 1–39). Isaiah offered hope of redemption and restoration of the nation through the Servant who would suffer on behalf of the people (the Suffering Servant, chapters 40–55). The last section of Isaiah (chapters 56–66) speaks of universal redemption.[2] Israel was not only to be redeemed, but God was going to redeem the entire human order. God's age of peace, healing, and wholeness would dawn throughout the world. The Messiah, the Anointed One, was to be the bearer and establisher of the new dominion and age. In Isaiah 61, the Messiah announces the good news of the new age to the poor and oppressed. God's dominion was now established, and all poverty, oppression, and captivity would be overcome.[3]

Due to her captivity, vassalage, and bondage, Israel was poor and brokenhearted. But Isaiah 61 proclaims that this was the year of God's favor, where God would set Israel free from her physical bondage, and set humankind free from the spiritual bondage that fosters the various forms of physical captivity. The messianic good news included salvation for the physically and spiritually poor. There would be judgment and vengeance for God's enemies, but for those who grieved in Zion, instead of the ashes of mourning on their foreheads, there would be the oil of gladness; instead of a spirit of despair and heaviness, they would wear a mantle of praise (Isaiah 61:1–3).

When Jesus chose Isaiah 61 and said, "Today this scripture has been fulfilled in your hearing," he was announcing that he was the Messiah, the herald of a new age. He was announcing that the law of Moses, the prophetic concern for justice and mercy, the longing of Israel for redemption and healing, and God's promise of a dominion of peace and love were all being fulfilled in him. He was announcing that God's dominion was established, and all oppression was overcome. The dominion of God had come, and the good news was that there was no more bondage of any kind, spiritual or physical, to those who became sons and daughters of God by faith in the victory of the Messiah.

When Jesus announced his mission in Luke 4, initially the people were amazed at the graciousness of his words and accepted his proclamation, but at a deeper level Jesus sensed their unbelief. They wanted him to perform signs and wonders to back up his claims about the dominion of God and prove that he was the Messiah. Jesus suggested that it was exactly because of their unbelief that they had not in the past received signs and would not receive any now. Jesus reminded them that God chose to work wonders with the Gentile widow at Zarephath and Naaman, the Syrian, because of Jewish unbelief. They became so enraged that they sought to kill him, but he went, as the text says, "on his way" (Luke 4:28–30).

The opposition of his home congregation was but a precursor for the kind of opposition Jesus would engender throughout his ministry. Jesus lived out the dominion of God: healing, teaching, counseling, and sharing God's love, but the forces of evil and unbelief rejected the dominion of God and sought to overcome the good news. The height of the opposition to the messianic announcement of God's dominion by Jesus was an attempt to end his mission through crucifixion. In the resurrection of Jesus, God vindicated Jesus and his announcement of the dominion of God. When God raised Jesus from the dead, the church understood that no power, no opposition, and no forces of evil could defeat the redemptive purposes of God in Jesus. The dominion of God had truly come! God, in the person of Jesus, established God's rule on earth, forever and ever.

Out of love and compassion for the dying and hurting people of the world, out of a passion that the benefits of God's rule be extended to everyone who desires to receive, Jesus commanded the church to proclaim the good news to all creation. Jesus mandated the church (Matthew 28:19), those who through the Spirit have appropriated the saving power of Christ, those who have accepted and believed in the rule of God's dominion in Christ, those who are the "celebrative community," to go forth and spread the good news of God's rule to the world.

THE CHURCH: THE CELEBRATIVE COMMUNITY

Whenever the good news of the gospel (the assurance of grace) is received and appropriated, celebration is the natural response. The story of Mary Magdalene best illustrates a natural celebrative response to the good news of the gospel.[4] In response to her healing, Mary Magdalene joined the "celebrative community" of people that followed Jesus, those who had a similar experience of the assurance of grace.

Scripture does not give us an account of the full conversion of Mary (Luke 8:2) or her acceptance of the good news, but there are some things that we can infer Mary Magdalene had seven demons within her, and we must assume that she was severely tormented. In the midst of her suffering, Jesus understood her condition and spoke comfortingly and lovingly with her. Before she knew it, Jesus brought those demons out of her, and she found herself healed.

The term is right, she found herself, because as far as she could tell, it was God's power that effected the healing. It was all so miraculous to her: when Jesus told the demons to come out, they came out. Jesus did not owe her anything and therefore was in no way beholden to her. But in all of her sorrow, pain, and grief, he so wonderfully helped her. Grace was the word that could be used to describe the means by which peace and healing had come to her. It was grace that allowed the good news (God's victory over demons) to touch her life.

She was so thankful for deliverance that she dedicated her life to Jesus. She followed him closely and became a member of the new community he was forming, a celebrative community of others he had helped. She gave considerably of her own means to support the community. The most obvious demonstration of her dedication was the fact that when things got the most difficult for Jesus, when most of the other disciples had deserted him, Mary Magdalene remained faithful and loyal. During the agony of crucifixion, Mary Magdalene was present at the foot of the cross, displaying an unashamed allegiance to Jesus. When Nicodemus and Joseph of Arimathea took the dead body from Pilate to bury it, Mary Magdalene was there, pained, yet steady and devoted. Even early on that Sunday morning she was grieving at the tomb and became the first to discover that Jesus was alive. Her thankfulness for the graciousness of the good news expressed itself in an unwavering commitment to the one who had set her free.

Her story was much the same as that of others in the community. Maybe they did not have demons, but the good news set them free from some form of oppression and bondage. And when they had been set free in accordance with God's will and grace, *their response was that of thanksgiving.* The church is the formation of community, the coming together of people who have accepted the good news, experience deliverance, and respond with thanksgiving and joy. This response is evidenced in the fact that so much of the language and experience of the New Testament church can be summed up as the movement from an inner experience of the assurance of grace to thanksgiving and celebration.[5] The church can be understood as the "celebrative community" because celebration and thanksgiving are the natural responses to the inner acceptance and appropriation of the good news. After this response to the acceptance of the good news, often one desires to become part of the community of people who have had the same experience of celebration.

The early church had a high consciousness of God's grace in their lives. Good news received as the assurance of grace will produce thanksgiving and joy, and this is the reason the climate of celebration is in and around every page of the New Testament. Even in the face of stern persecution, false prophets, church conflict, and many other adversities, the final word is always good news, celebration, and thanksgiving. Praise and thanksgiving form the melody line of the New Testament and find expression in many forms. For example, the hymns of the early church: the Magnificat of Mary: "My soul magnifies the Lord, and my spirit rejoices in God my savior" (Luke 1:46–55); the magnificent prologue to the Fourth Gospel: "In the beginning was the Word . . . and to all who received him, he gave power to become children of God" (John 1:1–14); the fervent admonition of Colossians 3:16: "Let the word of Christ dwell in you richly ... with gratitude in your heart sing psalms, hymns, and spiritual songs to God." In many other texts, the joy and thanksgiving are the same: the Christian manifesto in Romans 8:28: "All things work together for the good for those who love God, who are called according to God's purpose"; the inexpressible joy of reconciliation that comes from the lips of the father of the prodigal son: "For this son of mine was dead and is alive again; he was lost and is found!" (Luke 8:24); and the majestic celebration of Revelation 19, so fittingly captured in Handel's "Hallelujah Chorus" from *Messiah:* "For the Lord God Omnipotent reigneth ... King of Kings, Lord of Lords." If there were time and space, many, many more examples could be given. But the point is that the New Testament abounds with praise, glory, joy, and thanksgiving to God for victory in Jesus Christ. The Messiah had come and opened the new age. God poured forth gifts of salvation and liberation to the human order. The church was excited about it, and celebrated the grace that was at the center of their lives.[6]

This grace was so significant in their lives that much of the language used to describe the outpouring of celebrative emotions is, as John Koenig[7] points out, rooted in the stem of the word *grace.* The Greek word for grace is *charis,* with the root being *char* (pronounced *kyar*). The Greek word for joy is *chara;* rejoicing is *chario;* thanks is *eucharistia;* and gift is *charisma.* All these are rooted in *char,* all rooted in God's grace. These were the words coined to express the emotions and feelings that followed the reception of the good news. Celebration is not an optional emotion that we attach to the preaching of the gospel, but part of the natural experience of emotions that is at the heart of the gospel. This is not to suggest in some naive way that there were not problems in the celebrative community, but the final word was God's grace and God's love. No matter the problem, difficulty, or worry, God had overcome it in Jesus.

Jesus was careful to make sure that the community did not keep all this grace to themselves. The marvelous celebrative emotions were not an end in themselves; those who had received true grace were moved to extend the same grace to others. Jesus established that one of the central purposes of the true celebrative community was to go forth and share the good news with the world. The mission of the celebrative community is to proclaim that the dominion of death has been overcome and the dominion of God rules. This is a formidable task; how shall the church undertake it? How can a frail, human community share the good news with the world?

THE CHURCH: THE CHARISMATIC COMMUNITY

Now that we know that the mission of the church is to spread the good news, we must also understand how the Holy Spirit equips the church to carry out its assigned task. Though we have focused much on Jesus, a thread quietly woven throughout this tapestry of celebration is the Holy Spirit. The cornerstone of Christian living is grace: God met human beings in a condition of sin and oppression with good news and offered salvation. The Holy Spirit, through prompting and revelation, helps people to "see" and experience Jesus Christ as savior. There cannot be an experience of Christ as savior without an experience of the Holy Spirit. As James Dunn, who coined the term "charismatic community," has observed, the experience of the Spirit is the other side of the coin from faith in Christ (Romans 8:9; 2 Corinthians 1:21ff).[8]

We are now in the theology and thinking of Paul, who lifts for all to see the role of the Holy Spirit in the life of the celebrative community. For Paul, Christian community was the coming together of people who have the same experience of the Spirit moving them to witness to the victory of Christ and the dominion of God. The shared experience of the Spirit draws them together, inspires a common gratitude and purpose, and is the basis of their unity and oneness (1 Corinthians 12:13—one Spirit, therefore one body). Unity is the gift given by the Spirit by virtue of the saving experience. Thus it is clear how Paul in 2 Corinthians 13:13, 14 could speak of the communion of the Holy Spirit in which all members of the community participated by virtue of being saved by grace.

It is pivotal to Paul that all members of the community understand their participation in the Spirit, because to grasp this fully is to move from celebration to mission. As the shared experience of the

Spirit formed the community, the continuing manifestations or gifts (*charismata*) of the Spirit kept the community alive and gave impetus for their mission. The Holy Spirit helps to begin the community by assisting persons to "see" and experience Jesus, and keeps the community alive by the pouring forth of gifts; hence the church was the charismatic community. For Paul, as Dunn states, "*charisma* denoted any word or act that embodies grace (*charis*), which is a means of grace to another."[9] Spiritual gifts are the Holy Spirit giving grace to one individual, in order to grace others, for the purpose of "building up" the Body of Christ. All members of the community, by virtue of participation in the Spirit, are charismatic, receiving gifts to share with the community.

The Holy Spirit pours forth gifts for the church to achieve its mission. God gives gifts for the church to spread the good news. *Preaching is a spiritual gift given by the Holy Spirit to help the church and the world receive and celebrate the good news of Christ.* Through the spiritual gift of preaching, people are led to an experience of the assurance of grace, and the church fulfills its mission to proclaim the good news to the world.

PREACHING AS A SPIRITUAL GIFT

Paul does not directly refer to preaching as a spiritual gift. Paul gives lists of spiritual gifts (Romans 12; 1 Corinthians 12; Ephesians 4) and never lists what we know as preaching. Paul's literal discussion of gifts does not include preaching, but the spirit of Paul's teaching on gifts does. From basically three sources in the writings of Paul, we can infer that preaching is a spiritual gift: (1) 1 Corinthians 13 and 14, (2) Romans 10:13–15, and (3) Paul's understanding of spiritual gifts by definition.

First, we must look at 1 Corinthians 13 and 14. Earlier, we said Jesus was careful that the celebrative emotions did not become an end in themselves, but led to mission. Paul, in these two chapters, likewise adds a corrective to Corinthian abuse of the celebrative gifts. The Corinthian church eagerly desired the gift of speaking in tongues. They thought it was the highest and best gift, and were using it as a benchmark of spiritual superiority. Paul says in 1 Corinthians 14:1, "Pursue love and strive for the spiritual gifts, especially that you may prophesy." Paul corrects their spiritual superiority by suggesting that in following the way of love, prophecy, not tongues, is the gift to be most sought after. Prophecy edified believers and convinced unbelievers to come to Christ. Prophecy directed God's truth to people's lives for purposes of understanding and growth. From Paul's perspective, it was better publicly to prophesy so that others could be strengthened, than to be individually enthralled by the rapture of speaking in tongues.

A careful reading of the fourteenth chapter of 1 Corinthians illustrates that what Paul describes as prophecy could be considered preaching:

> Those who prophesy speak to other people for their *upbuilding, encouragement,* and *consolation* (v. 3, emphasis added).
>
> Those who speak in a tongue, build up themselves, but those who prophesy *build up* the church (v. 4, emphasis added).
>
> I thank God that I speak in tongues more than all of you; nevertheless, in the church I would rather speak five words with my mind to *instruct* others than ten thousand words in a tongue (vv. 18 and 19, emphasis added).
>
> But if all prophesy, an unbeliever or outsider who enters in is *reproved* by all and *called to account* by all. After the secrets of the unbeliever's heart are disclosed, that person will bow down before God and worship, declaring, "God is really among you" (vv. 24 and 25, emphasis added).

If we look carefully at the words that are italicized above, they are all words that could be descriptive of preaching—to upbuild, encourage, console, instruct, reprove, and call to account. Paul uses these terms to describe prophecy, but the effect of prophecy sounds much like the effect of preaching, especially when it leads to the repentance outlined in verses 24 and 25.

In discussion of 2 Corinthians 14, Ralph Martin aids our equation of prophesy to preaching by suggesting an alternative for the word *prophecy;* he renders it "proclaiming."[10] After establishing that prophesying and proclamation are interchangeable, Martin defines prophesying in much the same way that some would define preaching:

> So [Paul] highlights "prophesying" [proclaiming] (14:3), a spirit-gift that aims to bring God's truth to bear on human lives with a view to their *understanding* and *growth*.[11]

From this first source, we can clearly infer that for Paul preaching was a spiritual gift.

The second source that Paul uses to support that preaching is a spiritual gift is Romans 10:13–15:

> "Everyone who calls on the name of the Lord shall be saved." But how are they to call on one in whom they have not believed? And how are they to believe in one of whom they have never heard? And how are they to hear without someone to proclaim him [Jesus]? And how are they to proclaim him unless they are sent?

I want to concentrate on the word *sent*. What does the text mean when it says "sent"? The Greek word there is *apostolos;* one who is commissioned, one who is sent forth on a mission to act on behalf of another. *Apostolos* is used heavily in the Gospel of John to describe the intimate relationship of Jesus to God, the One who commissioned (John 10:39; 17:3). Jesus understood himself to be sent, which meant commissioned, called, and empowered for a mission to proclaim the dominion of God to the world. For Jesus, the concept of being sent implied relationship, dependence, empowering, commissioning, and ultimately absolute vindication, because those whom God sends are upheld by the power and authority of God.

This is the same criterion Paul is placing on the one who would preach. Preachers must be called and appointed by the Holy Spirit for the special task of proclaiming the good news. Preachers must have an intimate relationship with the Holy Spirit, by whom they are empowered, receive their commission, speak the word of God, and have confidence of vindication. Paul seems to be rhetorically asking in this Romans text, "How can we preach if we do not have a special relationship with the Holy Spirit? How can we preach if we have not been graced and gifted by the Holy Spirit for the task? How can we preach unless we are sent?" For Paul, it was impossible to truly preach the gospel and not be called, commissioned, empowered, *gifted*, and *sent*.

The last source from which we can conclude that preaching is a spiritual gift is Paul's definition of spiritual gift. Earlier in this chapter we quoted James Dunn's explanation that for Paul, "*Charisma* denoted any word or act that embodies grace (*charis*), which is a means of grace to another," and added our own interpretation that spiritual gifts are the Holy Spirit giving grace to one individual, in order to grace others, for the purpose of "building up" the Body of Christ. Paul, with this understanding of charisma, could expand the formal list of gifts to include any area of a believer's life that became a means of grace to other believers. Therefore, Paul concluded his "celibacy" was a spiritual gift because God used it to build up believers (1 Corinthians 7:7). By Paul's definition, preaching is a spiritual gift, because preaching is a word/act that embodies grace, which is a means to grace (build up) others.

I am hard pressed to believe, especially in light of the expansion beyond the formal lists, that Paul would not consider preaching a spiritual gift. *Preaching is a spiritual gift given by the Holy Spirit to help the church proclaim and celebrate the good news of Jesus Christ.* Preaching is a spiritual gift that leads people to an intuitive experience of the assurance of grace. The Bible witnesses to the fact that God in Christ overcame all evil, suffering, and death, and God spreads this good news through spiritually gifted, celebrative preaching.

We have looked closely at the good news, and at preaching as one of the ways God has gifted the church to spread the good news. In the next chapter, we will look closely at what preaching methods most effectively spread the good news. We will look at celebration as a method and vehicle the Holy Spirit effectively utilizes to bring the assurance of grace to the core belief of people. Let us now turn to look at "The Dynamics of Celebration."

3

The Dynamics of Celebration

We have established the biblical and theological foundation of the good news (the assurance of grace) in the person and ministry of Jesus the Christ. It is my thesis that celebration, moving at the level of emotional process, is the most effective method and vehicle to facilitate the assurance of grace in Jesus the Christ reaching the core belief of people. Our purpose in this chapter will be to elaborate upon this thesis and discuss the various dynamics that foster celebration in preaching. We must begin by defining celebration: *Celebration is the culmination of the sermonic design, where a moment is created in which the remembrance of a redemptive past and/or the conviction of a liberated future transforms the events immediately experienced.* The sermonic design is an emotional process that culminates in a moment of celebration when the good news (the assurance of grace) intensifies in core belief until one has received an inner assurance, affirmation, courage, and a feeling of empowerment. One experiences oneself as victorious (i.e., saved, set free, healed, encouraged, etc.) regardless of the external tragic circumstances of life.

We might use the civil rights struggle as a paradigm to view the empowering effects of celebrative emotional process. During the movement, many knew there were dogs, hoses, beatings, imprisonment, hatred, venom, and even death awaiting those who opposed segregation. In this violent climate, what made a nonviolent army believe they could bring segregation to its knees? A major contributing factor was the empowerment through celebration that manifested itself in the meetings held before and during the marches.

These meetings used celebration to create in the core belief of people an inner assurance of victory that became empowerment to march. Modeled after African American worship, the inspirational part of the meetings revolved primarily around three things: preaching, praying, and singing.[1] During the meetings, somebody would pray and address God with a celebrative and affirmative prayer such as:

> We give you thanks for giving us the sight to see a movement. A movement that cannot be stopped by all the forces of oppression. . . . You showed us that to be fully human means you are never satisfied as long as one of your brothers [sisters] is oppressed. That as long as one person is not free, no one is free. You showed us that we must fight for freedom and that we can't let nothing or no one "turn us around" . . . nothing can stop the truth . . . no matter what they try to do, that truth will make us free.[2]

After the prayer, they would sing songs of praise, victory, and testimony, often something like the classic African American folk song:

> When Israel was in Egypt land (Let my people go). Oppressed so hard they could not stand (Let my people go). Go down Moses, way down in Egypt's land. Tell ol' Pharaoh, Let my people go!
>
> No more shall they in bondage toil (Let my people go). Let them come out with Egypt's spoil (Let my people go). Go down Moses, way down in Egypt's land. Tell ol' Pharaoh, Let my people go![3]

After the singing, there would follow celebrative and liberating preaching like that of Martin Luther King Jr., who through the assurance of grace contained within his address would bring the entire meeting to a crescendo by saying:

> Well, I don't know what will happen now. We've got some difficult days ahead. But it doesn't matter with me now. Because I have been to the mountaintop. Like anybody I would like to live a long life. Longevity has its place. But I am not concerned about that now. I just want to do God's will. And He's allowed me to go up to the mountaintop. And I've looked over and seen the promised land. I may not get there with you. But I want you to know tonight, that we as a people will get to the promised land. And I'm happy tonight. I'm not worried

about anything. I'm not fearing any man. Mine eyes have seen the glory of the coming of the Lord.[4]

After experiencing the liberating power of this celebrative moment, the people marched, convinced that the power of God experienced in core belief was more powerful than the evil in the world. Celebration transformed their present reality, allowing them to face evil with courage and boldness. In the meetings, there was information and strategizing, to be sure, but the spirit of the meeting was that of celebration and victory. It was this celebrative spirit that they carried during the march, primarily voiced through singing and praying, that helped them to creatively confront and overcome evil.

Let's consider how the inspirational content of these meetings fit into the definition of celebration given at the beginning of the chapter:

Celebration is the culmination of the sermonic design where a moment is created in which the remembrance of a redemptive past . . .

The remembrance of a victory God won in the past was recalled by the words of the spiritual "Tell ol' Pharaoh, Let my people go."

. . . and/or the conviction of a liberated future . . .

The conviction of a liberated future was evidenced in the fervent prayer "that no matter what they try to do, the truth will make us free." This liberated future was based upon the core belief that, with the help of God, persistent and aggressive right would overcome all wrong.

. . . transforms the events immediately experienced.

Based on this remembrance of a redemptive past and conviction of a liberated future, they could overcome their fear and experience themselves as victorious, confirmed in the words from Dr. King's sermon, "I'm happy tonight. I'm not worried about anything. I'm not fearing any man. Mine eyes have seen the glory of the coming of the Lord."

Through this celebrative emotional process they experienced the power and truth of a liberating God. Having experienced transformation through celebration, they marched, and their feet changed the face of the evil system of segregation and influenced change throughout the world for years to come.[5]

Let us look at this definition of celebration from another sector of inquiry, from the system perspective of emotional process. When we give attention to emotional process and context, we could suggest that celebration is a reversal in the emotional field of the sermon that facilitates fresh encounter with truth. During the preaching of any sermon, an emotional field comes into existence, or what was pictured in the previous chapter as a "shared surface." This emotional field is shaped by the intersection of the preacher and the prepared sermon, the anticipation and projected expectations of the hearers, and the biblical text, which includes the work and purpose of the Holy Spirit. We shall say more about the Holy Spirit in the next section, but within this emotional field, the preacher executes reversals that do not rupture the shared surface of the field, and as a result helps people experience fresh encounter with truth. For example, the preacher during the civil rights movement does not ignore the reality of dogs, hoses, venom, and violence that are awaiting the nonviolent army. This reality is part of the shared surface of the emotional field; it is part of the preparation, anticipation, and projected expectation of the sermonic event. But in the context of that emotional field, the preacher proclaims the redemptive past and the liberated future, which functions as a reversal in the face of the evil experienced in the present. The reversal calls into question the patterns, beliefs, and perceptions circumscribed by the tragic reality of the present situation. The reversal offers a fresh sense of wonder about the imaginative possibilities of God. And because the imaginative possibilities of God intensified in core belief, they marched, went to jail, and defeated evil.

The civil rights movement is only a paradigm for what the Holy Spirit does each and every day in the lives of people through celebrative emotional process. Through the healing power of celebration, the Holy Spirit imparts a transformed present to people.

THE PREACHER AS CONSCIOUS CELEBRATOR

In the previous section it was stated that "the assurance of grace intensifies in core belief until one has received an inner assurance." The word *received* was carefully chosen, because it signifies that much of the transformative work of celebration is contingent upon the

Holy Spirit. The Holy Spirit causes and allows transformation to occur through celebration, and we preachers are junior partners and facilitators in celebrative emotional process. We assist the Spirit, but the work is that of the Holy Spirit. We are, to borrow a term from Cathy DeForest, "conscious celebrators."[6] Conscious celebration utilizes emotional process to project powerful celebrative and affirmative images in core belief, upon which the Holy Spirit "rides" to help people experience a transformed present.

We preachers are defined as conscious celebrators because we set out intending (praying and planning) for celebrative emotional process to occur. The preacher intends celebration by fashioning affirmative images that strike people in their inner core, and the Holy Spirit utilizes the images to help the hearer experience the transforming and liberating power of the gospel. Though true celebration is a gift of the Holy Spirit, celebration usually is not arbitrary and accidental. Celebration is the result of the preparation process by which the preacher comes to choose and present celebrative images upon which the Holy Spirit can ride to help people experience the assurance of grace. We shall say much more about the intentional preparation process of the celebrative sermon in chapter 4.

The African American preaching tradition of celebrative design has untold riches and experience in celebrative emotional process, affirmative images, and the practice of celebration. To help preachers become intentional and conscious celebrators, I would like to discuss several principles that emerge from and undergird the celebrative abundance of the African American preaching tradition. One principle within this tradition is so critical that I want to discuss it first and by itself—the concept of sense appeal.

Experiencing the Gospel and Sense Appeal

I became convinced of the arresting power of experiencing something several years ago as I sat in a theater watching the movie *The Color Purple*.[7] Before seeing the movie, I had read the book,[8] so I knew basically what was going to occur. The book and movie are about the struggle of Celie, the heroine, to gain dignity, respect, and personhood after a history of incest and abuse. In one scene of the movie, her abusive husband asks Celie to give him a shave. It is clear, as she brings the razor blade to his throat, that she wants to kill him. The slow and methodical way she maneuvers the razor made me frightfully aware that it was borderline as to whether or not she would. I had read the book, so I knew she was not going to do it. But the director of the movie, Steven Spielberg, so skillfully handled the images, music, and drama (the emotional process) of the scene that he *ordered my experience*, and I felt she was going to kill him even though I knew she was not. As I experienced the scene, the feelings of anxiety and fear, plus the sweat in my palms, overrode my intellectual knowledge. Believing that she was going to kill him, I felt the appropriate emotions, both terror that she would do it and satisfaction because revenge was being administered for the crimes inflicted. Through this movie experience, I became convinced of the arresting power of emotional process to order experience.

Convinced of the power of experience and emotional process over intellectual knowledge and cognitive assent, I began to reflect upon the difference between thinking about something and experiencing it. What is traditionally known as "thinking" usually involves a significant emotional and physical distance from a thing; one objectifies what one is thinking about, separates oneself and one's body from it, and dissects it for clarification and analysis. But when one experiences something, the body, emotions, and thinking are significantly involved. The body registers and confirms the reception of powerful stimuli and responds appropriately, for example, by sweating, feeling short of breath, or blinking away tears. The response is often automatic, below the level of conscious instruction and choice. This is not to suggest that thinking is not a critical part of the experiential process, but rational thinking does not dominate the process to force abstraction and emotional distance.[9] It is difficult to have an experience of something without thinking, but thinking that is experiential *involves* the emotions and the body, deemphasizing the rigid posture of abstraction, objectification, physical separation, and emotional distance. Experiential thinking operates from the perspective of what we might call "emotional objectivity." We have not looked at this possibility much in this culture, but it is possible to involve one's emotions and body *and* still be objective.[10]

When we involve our bodies and our emotions in our thinking, we are said to "experience" something. Jay E. Adams describes the process in the context of preaching:

> To experience an event in preaching is to enter into that event so fully that the emotions appropriate to that event are felt, just as if one were actually going through it. When a preacher says what he [she] relates in such a way that he [she] stimulates one or more of the five senses, thus triggering emotion, then the listener may be said to "experience" the event. In that way, the event will become "real" to him [her], which means it has become concretized (or personalized), memorable, and in the fullest sense of the word, understandable.[11]

When preaching effectively develops language and images that appeal to one or more of the five senses—sense appeal—the language and images beget identification. Once identification occurs, emotion is stirred and the listener becomes interested. When the preacher cultivates this interest, the listener is open in a fresh way to the preacher's message, open for reversal in the emotional field, and open to the gospel call for change. *The ability of the preacher to stir identification, emotion, and interest through sense appeal is what is meant by the term experiential preaching.*

If we want people to experience rather than solely intellectualize the good news, then we must construct sermons that help people see, taste, hear, touch, and feel the gospel. When we say that a sermon is boring or lifeless, at least some of what we mean is that it appealed to few if any of our senses. Without our senses being stirred, we do not have a means of identification, and if there is no identification, there is no release of emotion that sustains interest. And if our interest is not sustained, how will we respond to the reversals and challenge to change demanded by the gospel? Our intellects can be challenged without our senses being stirred, but that will not be enough to empower people to respond to the gospel invitation for change.

Before we discuss some of the techniques that make for effective use of sense appeal, it is important to emphasize the critical fact that *people rarely experience the sermon if the preacher does not experience it first.*

The preacher must prepare and shape *the sermon and the preacher's self* from the perspective of experiential preparation (of which I shall say more in chapter 4). The preacher who would focus on the following techniques alone, and miss the fundamental truth that the preacher must be an "experiential self," will find it tremendously difficult to help people experience the sermon, despite the practice of technique.

The first technique of the experiential self is the use of metaphorical language laden with sense-arousing images. The Bible is full of descriptive and imaginative metaphorical language and images that stimulate the senses. Notice the images and language and the senses that are stirred through several biblical passages:

> Even youths will faint and be weary, and young men will fall exhausted, but those who wait for the Lord will renew their strength. They shall mount up with wings like eagles; they shall run and not be weary, they shall walk and not be faint. (Isaiah 40:30–31)

> Indeed, the word of God is living and active, sharper than any two-edged sword, piercing until it divides soul from spirit, joints from marrow; it is able to judge the thoughts and intentions of the heart. (Hebrews 4:12–13)

> I saw one like the Son of Man, clothed with a long robe and with a golden sash across his chest. His head and hair were white as wool, white as snow; his eyes were like a flame of fire, his feet were like burnished bronze, refined as in a furnace, and his voice was like the sound of many waters. (Revelation 1:12)

The sense appeal of these texts is very vivid and gripping—"they will *soar* on *wings* like *eagles*," "*sharper* than any *two-edged sword, piercing* until it *divides soul from spirit*," "his feet were like *burnished bronze, refined* as in a *furnace*, and his voice was like *the sound of many waters*." The language is sense-arousing with vivid and picture-like imagery that stirs identification, emotion, and interest. I believe that certain scriptural passages have become the most popular and meaningful passages to congregations over the years because of the vivid metaphorical language and sense-arousing imagery they employ. When a text connects intimately with the senses, it becomes, as Adams says, "concretized (or personalized), memorable, and in the fullest sense of the word, understandable."[12] The biblical texts and sermons that connect most vividly with the senses of the listeners are the texts and sermons people remember and quote and that have the best chance to be lived.

It is not necessary to be a great poet or storyteller to use metaphorical language and sense-arousing imagery effectively; it is a skill that preachers can develop, and there is good help available. An excellent source and training tool is the chapter "Gathering Storytelling Materials," in Adams's *Preaching with Purpose*.[13] In that chapter Adams challenges us all when he says:

> You do not have to look very far for your material (illustrations). Wherever you are at the moment, look around you. All the material you need for the next ten years could be found by sitting right there—in your study, or wherever you are—if you will only fully open all your senses to it, and set your mind to work on chiseling what you find there into usable shapes.[14]

Metaphorical language is in us all; it has to be nurtured, cultivated, developed, and released.[15] Many of the persons we consider great preachers worked hard to develop the skill and knack of metaphorical language and chiseling things into "usable shapes."

Recently in one of my preaching classes there was a student who the entire quarter expressed anxiety about having to preach a sermon to end the class. Nervousness about this assignment was not, of course, unusual, except that one week before she was scheduled to preach, she raised the concern again, painstakingly detailing her own sense of overall inadequacy to receive God's call to ministry, and therefore, questionable competency for the preaching task. I decided to challenge her rather than display empathy for her concerns.

I remembered the jingle from a very popular television commercial, "Raise your hands! Raise your hands, if you're sure!" I remembered the commercial and the jingle because it had such great sense appeal. I nonanxiously said, "There will come a time in your life when you must raise your hands if you are sure." I was implying that there are critical times in life when, despite our fears, we must declare ourselves, take a stand, and choose a position. It seemed to me that the sermon next week was just such a moment for her, and she had a position to take. The tone of my communication suggested that I was not stressed in the least about her misgivings, or her upcoming choice. I was absolutely certain that within the next week she would make the most appropriate decision. I was at ease if she preached, and at ease if she did not preach.

What she had expected was that I would anxiously attempt to convince her that she was called, and convince her that preaching was part of that call. The commercial and the jingle, the raw material of everyday life, was the vehicle to reverse the content and help her experience a fresh sense of wonder about her own apprehension. It so happened that she *was* sure, preached the next week, and did a wonderful job. Life is full of sense-appealing usable shapes that can be carved into images that vividly connect with the senses of the listeners, and help people experience fresh encounter.

Besides the technique of metaphorical language and image, we must use our bodies to appeal to the senses with tone/sounds and gestures. Many of us limit the effectiveness of the messages we are delivering by being inhibited in our use of tone and sound. Jesus used tone and sound freely as a natural part of his preaching and teaching ministry. When he used "woe" in Matthew 23, it was more of an exclamation or groan of pain (like our "ouch") than a word. Watch and listen to master preachers and storytellers. Listen to the way they captivate an audience with free use of sound. If you watch and listen carefully, you will discover that they are experiencing the sermon or story as they deliver it. My guess is that because the sermon or story is an experience for them, they experience the freedom to employ whatever tones and sounds are natural and appropriate to the communication of the message. *We could probably be as effective if we fully engaged our bodies, thinking, and emotions in the sermonic preparation and delivery process, and the sermon was an experiential encounter for us.*

Many of us are also inhibited with our bodies. We often forget that we are being watched as well as heard. And in this culture of the visual (video games, video music, etc.), if we are going to communicate powerfully, we must have an effective visual presentation. This does not mean that we must choreograph our messages. One of the worst things in preaching is when either gesture, body movement, or tone and sound come off as wooden and staged. But we must take care to realize that our gestures, our facial expression, our tones/ sounds, our bodily movement, and our posture $\lceil$*stimulate or limit the operation of sense appeal in the emotional field.* $\rceil$

I rarely write in the margin of my preaching manuscript "Get loud here!" or "Raise your hands here!" because when the sermon is being experienced by the preacher as it is preached, the experience itself dictates the appropriate tones, sounds, and gestures. When the preacher is experiencing the sermon and says, "The news of his death took all of my breath away," then a natural move might be to place the hands to the throat, demonstrating loss of breath. The gesture moves the language to another dimension of sense appeal in the body of the listener. Because the gesture originates from the preacher's experience (body, emotions, and thinking) of the sermon, it reaches the experience (body, emotions, and thinking) of the hearers.

Much more needs to be said about the use of sense appeal. This is a small beginning, but it does call attention to the fact that we must give much more concern to *experiencing* the gospel. This beginning raises significant questions about our dependence on cognitive process and underscores the fact that inattention to emotional process based in sense appeal limits the effectiveness of our communication.

Sense Appeal and Emotional Process

Jay E. Adams believes that the most effective preachers have mastered the art of sense appeal.[16] What Adams suggests is true, but it is not just sense appeal that makes a preacher effective; rather it is the fact that sense appeal is a gateway to the emotional process of the sermon. Sense appeal is the physical doorway that allows the preacher to move within the scope of the emotional field of the sermon. Once the preacher has access to the emotional field, the preacher can execute reversals that make for fresh encounter. So that our meaning is clear, let us go back and talk again about the emotional field.

We said earlier that during the sermonic event, an emotional field comes into existence shaped by the preparation of the preacher, the expectations of the hearers, and the purpose of the Holy Spirit in the text. We talked about this emotional field as a "shared surface"; within this shared surface the preacher executes reversals that do not rupture the field and thereby sets the stage for fresh encounter. The sermon is an emotional field that could be discussed by analogy to a magnetic field or gravitational field.

A field is an environment or force that is not made up of physical matter but only comes into existence when physical matter gets close to physical matter. When the physical matter and substance of the planets within the solar system come into a certain relationship with one another, a gravitational field comes into existence that affects the behavior and movement of every planet within the field. The field is not made of physical matter, but it cannot come into existence unless physical matter comes into relationship with matter. But once the field comes into existence, it has more power to influence the planets than the planets have to influence the field, though the relationship of the planets brought the field into existence in the first place. Once the field comes into existence, it has properties, principles of organization, and gravitational effect of its own that influence everything within the field.

It is through sense appeal that the physical matter (body, thinking, and emotions) of the preacher engages the physical matter (body, thinking, and emotions) of the listener, and the physical matter (body, thinking, and emotions) of the text. Upon the engagement of the physical matter of preacher, hearer, and text, the emotional field comes into existence. Once the emotional field exists, the Holy Spirit comes center stage to influence everything within the field. The celebrative gravitational effect of the Holy Spirit has more power to influence the participants in the field than the participants have to influence the field. The Holy Spirit utilizes the affirmative gravitational power of the emotional field to order the experience of the preacher and listener. When we suggest that the Holy Spirit "transforms the events immediately experienced," we mean that within the celebrative emotional field of the gospel, the Holy Spirit gives new order to the experience of the preacher and listener through the text. The Holy Spirit transforms reality within the celebrative field, but the field only comes into existence based upon the physical relationship of text, preacher, and hearer. Once the field comes into existence, the Holy Spirit is the principle of organization that directs everything within the field towards the hope, courage, empowerment, and celebration contained within the gospel.

By virtue of the fact that the preacher and the people gather together with a text, every sermon to some extent or another has sense appeal and forms an emotional field. But for the preacher who would manage celebrative emotional process, the senses must be fully and effectively engaged. The preacher who would direct celebrative emotional process must personally experience the text and sermon in the preparation process, and then by invitation offer that celebrative experience to the listeners. When the listeners offer their experience (body, thinking, and emotions) to the text and sermon, a powerful celebrative emotional field comes into existence that the Holy Spirit uses to transform both preacher and listener.

PRINCIPLES OF CELEBRATIVE DESIGN

As pointed out earlier, the African American preaching tradition of celebrative design has untold riches and experience in celebrative emotional process, affirmative images, and the practice of celebration. Through close inspection and identification of several principles and characteristics that undergird celebrative design, we can tap into this rich legacy for helping in our conscious attempts to facilitate celebrative emotional process. Several principles to be mentioned here have been discussed previously, and many are grounded in the concept of sense appeal and experience that has occupied center stage within this chapter. But we enumerate them to bring to the conscious and intentional level some of the dynamics that operate within the emotional field of the African American celebrative sermon. We will develop seven principles of celebrative design.

(1) *Celebration Treats Evil as Experiential Encounter.* The existential plight of African American people forced the preacher and the people to move beyond sin, evil, and suffering as primarily intellectual concepts and philosophical categories. African Americans interpreted their experience of slavery, segregation, and racism as evil that was deeply and concretely experienced in their bodies, emotions, and thinking.

The reality of evil was seen, felt, tasted, heard, and touched, and therefore the philosophical and metaphysical foundation of evil was *obvious*. It was not that African Americans did not have a metaphysical and philosophical base, but the experience of evil was so vivid that, as Walter Wink says, "the issue is not whether there is a metaphysical entity called Satan, but how we are to make sense of our actual experiences of evil."[17] It is the same for any race, nationality, or people: actual experiences of evil take place within the base of experiential encounter, that is, evil is concretely experienced through the senses and registers in the body, thinking, and emotions. The African American preacher addressed evil experientially because evil was so intimately and tangibly experienced in the senses of the people.

While the general rule is that African American preachers experientially address evil, I have heard many boring, unimaginative sermons from African American preachers who were preaching to people who were intimately experiencing evil (like addiction, poverty, crime, abuse, etc.). These preachers were discussing evil exclusively in philosophical concepts and intellectual categories, missing the experience of the people entirely. I have wondered about this incongruity and have decided that to preach experientially, the preacher must identify with the people irrespective of the race, class, or gender of the preacher or the people. Preachers who identify with the suffering of the people do not preach about evil in the abstract. It is the height of nonidentification and denial to deliver sermons in philosophical categories to listeners who know intimately and concretely that sin and evil are painfully and frightfully experienced by the senses.

2. Celebration Is the Experiential Assurance of Grace that Overcomes Evil. If the primary experiences of evil are experiential encounter, then rational discourse, metaphysical and philosophical explanations alone are inadequate to cope with evil. African Americans outlasted evil not through intellectual constructs but through an experience of the assurance of grace contained within the gospel. African Americans affirmed the lesson taught by the friends of Job:[18] those that suffer deeply and profoundly are comforted not by with intellectual explanation and theological justification of suffering but by an experiential encounter with the assurance that God is with them in the suffering, and in God, the suffering is overcome (the gospel).

Within the tradition of celebrative design, the goal of the African American sermon is to help people experience the assurance of grace that is the gospel. But this goal can never be achieved if the good news is established as an intellectual and philosophical abstraction separated from the experience (senses) of the people. Although the assurance of grace has a theological, philosophical, and metaphysical base, for the African American preacher that assurance must be grounded in the senses and experiences of the people. The assurance of grace must be seen, tasted, heard, felt, and touched. The good news must register in the body, thinking, and emotions of the preacher and people. Celebrative design clearly rests on the belief that concrete and intimate evil requires concrete and intimate encounter with the good news.

3. *Celebration Is a Positive Influence on Behavior.* Celebration helps the preacher motivate people through the positive reinforcement of the gospel, which means people are motivated by the affirmative means of love, joy, hope, and celebration. Every sermonic design and method has implicit or explicit assumptions of specific influence on the behavior of the listener. Some preachers believe that the means to influence behavior is through:

- intellectual explanations: so the sermon informs and appeals to reason

- emotional catharsis: so the sermon appeals to the emotions of the listener

- moral suasion: the preacher tells the congregation how they ought to behave

- utilitarianism: lives would be happier if the congregation emulated the gospel

- guilt and condemnation: if people do not change, then God will punish

Most preachers might use any and all of these in any given sermon to attempt to influence behavior, but celebrative emotional process is the highest and best method for influencing the behavior of people with the gospel, because celebration motivates through positive reinforcement of the gospel within the emotional field.

Celebrative design has learned that if the preacher helps people experience a redemptive past and/or a liberated future, then people have been offered the best motivation to behave in new ways. The sheer joy and power of experiencing a redemptive past/liberated future is the best motivator to influence behavior.

Motivating people externally through negative means and coercion (manipulation, fear, guilt, etc.), does not produce lasting change. Often it generates resistance and resentment among congregation members that will eventually explode in harmful ways, a cycle that is much too prevalent in churches today. Celebrative emotional process frees us to break this cycle. Within the African American celebrative sermon people are motivated by the positive and healing power of the gospel, which does not coerce, manipulate, or motivate through fear. The experience of celebrative design is that people will recall and practice much more of what they have celebrated. People respond better when motivated and inspired by the affirmative means of the gospel—love, joy, hope, and celebration.

4. *Celebrative Design Is Immediate.* Because of the effective utilization of sense appeal, preaching within the tradition of celebrative design is immediate, which means there is no historical distance between the Bible, the preacher, and the listeners. The sermon is experiential encounter, to the extent that the Bible is taking place in the midst of congregational life, and the people are included in the unfolding drama. When Jesus heals blind Bartimaeus, the people are right there as eyewitnesses watching it happen and develop. Depending on the text, Moses, David, Ruth, Daniel, Solomon, Mary Magdalene, Paul, and Jesus himself are in the assembly, easily seen, heard, reached, touched, and understood. The African American preaching tradition, in the words of Keith D. Miller, telescopes history, replacing chronological time with a form of sacred time. Miller says:

> This substitution enabled Old Testament characters to become slaves' immediate predecessors and contemporaries as they freely mingled their own experiences with those of Daniel, Ezekiel, Jonah, Joshua, and Moses. Slaves could vividly project Old Testament figures into the present because their expansive uni-

verse encompassed both heaven and earth and merged the biblical past with the present.[19]

I heard James A. Forbes Jr. recount that Gardner C. Taylor[20] preached the story of the prodigal son so effectively that at the end of the story, when the boy was on the road coming home, Taylor pointed to the back of the church and said, "There he is now, coming up the road!" Forbes says he turned around and actually saw the prodigal son coming up the road. Taylor's sense appeal preaching was just that immediate.

5. *Celebrative Design Utilizes Self-Identification and Self-Recognition.* The sermon that shapes and becomes an experiential encounter produces self-identification/self recognition. That is, one can identify and recognize oneself in the sermon/text, and experience through that identification the body, emotions, and thinking appropriate to the text. The emotions, attitudes, and behavior of the good Samaritan, for example, are so vivid and stimulating to the senses of the listener that the listener in a vicarious way becomes the good Samaritan. When the parable is preached in this experiential manner, *we* find the person on the road, beaten, cut, and bruised, *we* feel the compassion and pity, and *we* take the person to the inn. The Bible is not just happening for us, but to us and in us.

A vivid example of self-identification/recognition appeared earlier in this chapter when we discussed the heroine, Celie, of the book and movie *The Color Purple.* Spielberg's movie treatment of Celie's potential response in the shaving scene triggered, through my self-identification/self-recognition, the places in my life where I have been angered by mistreatment. My identification with Celie helped me experience the scene, and added to the intensity that had the effect of overriding my knowledge of what would occur next. Despite the fact that I had read the book and knew she would not kill him, I vicariously felt the appropriate emotions as if she would. The preacher experientially and insightfully preaches the text, and the listeners supply the details from their own lives that allow for self-recognition and self-identification.

6. *Celebration Is Facilitated by a Conscious Celebrator.* Within the tradition of celebrative design the preacher serves as leader, designer,

and catalyst to the experience of celebration. By virtue of experiential preparation of the celebrative sermonic design, the preacher has already experienced the good news of the sermon. Therefore, the preacher is the first into the waters of celebration, and invites the congregation to wade in as well. Based upon the preacher's experiential invitation, several accept, and celebration becomes a contagion that spreads until we find many members of the congregation in the waters. Celebration usually will not occur if the preacher/designer/catalyst does not celebrate and wade in first. As we stated earlier, if the preacher does not experience celebration in the preparation and delivery of the sermon, then in all likelihood the people will not experience celebration either.

7. Celebrative Design Is Carefully Timed to Crescendo. Celebrative design has a natural order and movement that establishes proper placement and sequencing of sermonic material so that the sermon culminates in the celebrative moment. We all understand that music has planned order and movement until it culminates with a signature ending that announces the end of the piece and reinforces the musical intent already expressed in the performance of the music. Celebrative design has likewise understood that the sermon, as a work of homiletical art, must place and sequence materials within the sermon so that they climax with a signature ending that is celebrative. This signature ending announces the end of the sermon and reinforces what has already been preached (more will be said of this in chapter 5).

If we are going to be conscious celebrators, then we must employ these principles of celebrative design. Tested through time in the history and experience of African American celebrative preaching, they have proven to sustain and empower people.

EXPERIENCING THE GOSPEL AND TRADITIONAL FORMS

It is important to clarify the distinction between celebrative design and the traditional preaching forms and categories of topical/expository/textual sermons.[21] This is necessary because many readers are familiar with these categories of sermons and may want to know what place they occupy in celebrative design.

Within celebrative design there is little discussion of these traditional forms: celebrative design is more concerned with experiencing the gospel. If one is going to preach an expository sermon, then it had better be an experiential expository sermon, or it will not matter. If one is going to preach a topical sermon, then one had better make sure it is experientially topical to have the most impact upon the listener. If one is going to preach an exegetical sermon, if it is not experientially exegetical, then it will probably seem boring and lifeless to the congregation.

In the recent past of Western homiletics, the primary mode in which these traditional forms have been used has been the method of rational discourse. The common basis of appeal underneath the topical/expository/textual sermon was to the rational intellect of the listener. We have suggested that the appeal to the rational intellect alone is not sufficient to get the gospel heard today. Henry H. Mitchell lists several forms (genres) used by celebrative design that have not been considered traditional, i.e., narrative, dialogue, character sketch, group study, etc.[22] Celebrative design can use both traditional and nontraditional forms, but the bottom line is to generate an experiential encounter in the sermon.

The preaching of Jesus was experiential, and because the listener was experiencing the gospel, it did not matter if it was textual or topical or expository. What was important to the listener was the fresh insight and the novel rush of emotion that followed Jesus' ability to place gospel truth in the container of sense appeal. Truth wrapped in the container of sense appeal helps people *experience* the gospel and the challenge of change requested by the gospel. I close with Jesus' masterful use of experiential technique:

> Therefore I tell you, do not worry about your life, what you will eat or what you will drink, or about your body, what you will wear. Is not life more than food, and the body more than clothing? Look at the birds of the air; they neither sow nor reap nor gather into barns, and yet your heavenly Father feeds them. . . . And why do you worry about clothing? Consider the lilies

of the field, how they grow; they neither toil nor spin, yet I tell you that Solomon in all his glory was not clothed like one of these. . . . But strive first for the kingdom of God and its righteousness, and all these things will be given to you as well. (Matthew 6:25–33)

In the next chapter, we turn to specific methodology for designing the celebrative sermon and seek to grapple with the question, "How does one design a sermon that celebrates?"

4

Designing for Celebration

The most difficult chapter in any text on homiletics is the one in which the author must set down specific methodology to achieve what has been defined as good preaching. It is much easier to define celebration than to describe the steps in preparing a celebrative sermon. So how do we design for celebration? How do we bring the experience of celebration into the steps and stages of intentional homiletic method and preparation? How do we consciously design a sermon that helps people experience a redemptive past/liberated future? The place to begin is to look at the sermon from a systems perspective.

SYSTEMS THINKING AND THE CELEBRATIVE SERMON

It is critical to begin with a shift to a systems perspective because a systems perspective allows us to distinguish the preparation of the emotional context from the preparation of content. Most homiletic method focuses on the preparation of content with little attention to the emotional process, but intentional preparation of the emotional context is primary to the celebrative sermon. In order to examine intentional preparation of the emotional context, we must return to thinking expressed in the first and the third chapters.

In chapter 1, "Celebrative Design and Emotional Process," we were clear that communication is not exclusively a cerebral process. Viewing communication as a cerebral process leads to a focus on words, logic, ideas, exegesis, diction, etc.—in other words, *content*. To a significant degree, however, communication is an emotional phenomenon, and therefore paying attention to the emotional context of communication is more important than the choosing of right words. Good preaching is a function of very careful and deliberate attention to the emotional context into which content is placed.

In chapter 3, "Dynamics of Celebration," we defined celebration as the culmination of the sermonic design, where a moment is created in which the remembrance of a redemptive past and/or the conviction of a liberated future transforms the events immediately experienced. When we say that celebration is the culmination of the sermonic design, we mean that in any sermon, "emotional process, which takes time, always has the power to override diction, or ideas, or to give them eloquence."[1] We mean that good preaching is the *right content* delivered at the *right moment*, with the *right sense of timing*. We mean that the focus is not exclusively on the content of the sermonic system, i.e., words, introduction, conclusion, etc., but on the emotional process that governs and orders the content. We are not just shaping information to be contained in the sermon, but looking at the principles of organization that give the information meaning. Celebrative emotional process utilizes these organizing principles to manage the content of the sermon upward to the goal of celebration. We begin to discern these principles with a look at the pattern of situation-complication-resolution.

For centuries upon centuries and generations upon generations, human beings have noticed a pattern in life: one experiences a situation, there occurs some complication of that situation, and then invariably there is some kind of resolution of the complication. This pattern is so pervasive in the human experience that it has become embedded in the intuitive aspect of human awareness as an instinct or a form. I believe the form to be intuitive because it is found in human civilization worldwide, from the earliest creation myths of the ancient world, to the plays of Sophocles, to the parables of Jesus, to the tragedies of Shakespeare, to the slave folktales of Brer Rabbit and Brer Fox, to modern television sitcoms, to multimillion-dollar movie productions, to the sound bytes of politics and political campaigns. One of the most powerful constructs in human communication is the intuitive form of situation-complication-resolution.

The homiletic genius demonstrated in "Uncle Wash's Funeral" in chapter 1 is clearly connected to the intuitive form of situation-complication-resolution. The intuitive form can be clearly discerned in the story:

Situation: Uncle Wash was a blacksmith, church member, and a good Christian man, in that he used the hammer and tongs to help people from miles and miles around;

Complication: Uncle Wash was accused and convicted of stealing, went to jail, contracted consumption, came home, and died;

Resolution: Uncle Pompey preached the funeral and gave the assurance of grace that Uncle Wash was in heaven, because there were plenty of folk in heaven who went to jail, among them Paul and Silas.

It is the skillful utilization of situation-complication-resolution that helps to make "Uncle Wash's Funeral" such a powerful narrative. Throughout the entire history of the human family, those who would create powerful communicative expression have recognized and used this form.

Understanding the intuitive form of situation-complication-resolution leads us to the awareness of plot. From the perspective of emotional context, plot is developed when the complication gets introduced, and suspense is added to the drama. Suspense spurs the listener, through growing excitement and interest, to seek equilibrium when confronted with the complication. The complication is the presentation of situations, circumstances, or facts that throw the listener off balance and cause a feeling of anxiety/uneasiness. The human personality naturally seeks balance, stability, and equilibrium, and it is the management of this anxiety that keeps the listener engaged. Suspense is necessary for people to listen. *Therefore, the first organizing principle of the emotional context of the celebrative sermon is the introduction of suspense.* The preacher must introduce and manage suspense to keep the listener actively engaged in the sermon.

Human personality not only requires the introduction and management of suspense to keep listening, but naturally requires resolution of the suspense. The natural human need for equilibrium causes people to intensely invest in the sermon looking for the resolution of the presented suspense. When suspense is properly planned and focused, the sermonic design resolves the suspense with the gospel, and people experience a sense of completion or resolution that makes the sermon worth the hard work of listening. The sermon raises suspense, names it, and helps people experience it, then resolves the suspense in light of the gospel. When resolution/celebration occurs, the sense of completion leads to a shift and transformation of the hearer's perspective, attitude, feeling, and commitment that will come to full fruition in the last component of the emotional context—celebration. Thus, *the second organizing principle of the emotional context of the celebrative sermon is the resolution of suspense.* If listeners are going to experience a sense of completion that can lead to celebration, then the preacher must resolve the presented suspense.

The intuitive form of situation-complication-resolution is so deeply embedded in human awareness that whenever a situation and its complication are announced, people naturally look for resolution. The celebrative sermon is organized to move with and build upon this natural inclination for resolution, but adds tremendous intensity to the resolution with celebration. At the point where the situation-complication is resolved by the gospel, celebration kicks in to joy-fully and ecstatically reinforce the resolution. The reinforced resolution, with the help of the Holy Spirit, intensifies in core belief to the degree that it can shift perspective, attitude, feeling, and commitment. *The third organizing principle of the emotional context of the celebrative sermon is the celebration of the resolution of the suspense.* The preacher must celebrate the gospel resolution to the complication.

As an example of this third organizing principle, let's look closely at how Uncle Pompey's sermon resolves the situation-complication of the Uncle Wash narrative:

> *Situation:* Uncle Wash was a good Christian man, and fulfilled Christ's command to feed the hungry and clothe the naked.
>
> *Complication:* Uncle Wash was accused and convicted of stealing, went to jail, contracted a disease, and died.
>
> *Resolution (Gospel Assurance):* Because Paul and Silas are in heaven, it is obvious that being in jail on earth does not keep one out of

heaven. Heaven is full of people that have been arrested, including Uncle Wash.

Celebration: Uncle Wash climbs Jacob's ladder and is welcomed into heaven by the "dyin' thief." The "fountain filled with blood" makes it possible for thieves to get to heaven.

Uncle Pompey's sermon is based on the intuitive form of situation-complication-resolution, and the resolution has been intensified with celebration to reach core belief.

Once the gospel resolves the complication, the sermon shifts to the high moment, the apex, the zenith of the entire sermonic design—celebration. The stage of celebration begins when Uncle Pompey introduces Jacob's ladder, and it is at the pinnacle of celebration that the narrator says:

An' when they got to singin' 'bout the dyin' thief in heaven, an' they seen the 'surance of grace that was in it, they like to never quit praisin' God.

It is at the place of celebration that the sermonic system culminates, and persons are helped to experience the transforming power of the Holy Spirit. When content is employed with this deeper understanding of emotional process, the celebrative sermon has the ability to shift and transform the hearer's perspective, attitude, feeling, and commitment.

If the preacher would preach a celebrative sermon, the preacher must intentionally prepare the emotional context of the sermon. To prepare the emotional context is to grapple with the introduction of suspense, the resolution of suspense, and the celebration of the resolution. At the same time, consideration must be given to the resistance that is latent in any attempt to communicate.

ANALYZING THE RESISTANCE

There is something fundamental in human nature, traditionally categorized as sin or evil, that resists truth, growth, maturity, and celebration. Therefore, resistance can be defined as the denial of truth, aversion to growth, refusal of maturity, and negation of celebration that is latent within the emotional field of any attempt to preach or communicate. Within the celebrative sermonic system, there are three forms of resistance that must be addressed: structural resistance, relational resistance, and resistance to maturity.

Structural resistance is resistance fostered by structural defects in the sermonic design. If the sermonic design has a minimum of structural flaws, then suspense is properly planned, focused, and resolved, and celebration naturally occurs. Unplanned suspense, however, creates excessive tension within listeners, and has the effect of breaking down the upward movement of the system toward resolution and celebration. Structural resistance arising from the introduction of unplanned suspense can occur when:

1. the preacher is an expert at analyzing the problem (the bad news) but a novice at concrete gospel solutions that give people hope, and therefore the sermon has more bad news than good news;

2. the lack of clarity, purpose, and focus takes listeners down side roads, and listeners notice they are miles off any course that the sermon might be traveling to resolution;

3. the purpose of the sermon is unclear, and therefore listeners miss what they are to do or be as a result of the sermon, and how they are being invited to biblical change.

These kinds of structural defects in the sermonic system, often fostered by the preacher, increase anxiety and break down the upward movement to resolution and celebration. Later in this chapter, we will, through the vehicle of the Preaching Worksheet, discuss planning measures preachers can take to minimize structural resistance.

The second kind of resistance is labeled *relational resistance* because communication is an emotional process that depends heavily on the relationship between the parties trying to communicate. In every relationship, there are emotional barriers that prevent people from hearing each other. Normally we pay little attention to these emotional barriers, and assume that communication is about content— the right words, ideas, and diction. The success of communication, however, has to do with the appropriate content delivered in the right emotional envelope. Friedman suggests that the emotional context, and the barriers within the emotional context, are directly affected by three critical relational factors—distance, direction, and anxiety:[2]

Direction. In any attempt to communicate, a fundamental question must be asked: Are the parties moving toward each other, away from each other, or standing in neutral corners? *People can hear each other only when they are emotionally moving toward each other.* If the preacher would get the message heard, the preacher must maintain the kind of presence that maximizes the potential that listeners will move toward the preacher.

Distance. When we move toward each other to communicate, there is the danger that we move toward each other so quickly and tightly that we lose the ability to think clearly. *Clear thinking in relationships has to do with emotional distance that fosters independent space.* The preacher must maintain the kind of presence that communicates sufficient distance to enable each listener to think clearly as an independent self.

Anxiety. Anxiety functions as static in the communication system between two people. *The more anxious people are in their relationship, the more static there is in the communication line, and the less they can hear each other.* If the preacher would get the message heard, the preacher must maintain the kind of presence that lowers the anxiety in the emotional field.

We must face the fact that an important component in communication is the relationship between the preacher and the people, and that this relationship is affected by the relational factors of distance, direction, and anxiety. The preacher must cultivate a relational presence that allows people to move toward the preacher, allows enough distance for clear thinking, and allows for the lowering of anxiety to help the message get heard. Preaching has a great deal to do with the kind of relational presence the preacher brings to the sermon, as well as the right and appropriate content.

This leads us to the third category of resistance, *resistance to maturity.* Maturity is defined here as the willingness to take responsibility for one's own relationship with God, and the life, decisions, choices, and actions that flow from that relationship. Many people, even including some preachers, are unwilling to assume such responsibility, devising clever techniques and maneuvers to avoid it.

One of the classic techniques to avoid maturity is to deify and overvenerate the preacher. Deifying the preacher is often used as a defense against the fragility, ambiguity, and uncertainty of many choices and relationships in life. To relieve the anxiety that this ambiguity causes, some make the preacher larger than life and insist that the preacher offer pat answers to life's difficult and complex issues. Rather than take personal responsibility for the ambiguity in many of the choices of life, some people will demand certainty from the Bible and the church.[3]

In such a climate of overveneration, the critical question for the preacher is: How does one speak for God, and not end up with responsibility for the lives and salvation of people? How does one preach the word of God and then diminish, so that the encounter of dialogue is between God and the listener? How does the preacher express the sentiment of God, and ensure that healing is more dependent on the functioning of the person in conversation with God than on the functioning of the preacher? These are difficult questions, because the preacher is the spokesperson for God and theologian for the church, a role that carries tremendous amounts of respect and authority. When the inherent respect and authority of the preacher's role get mixed up with the need of some in the congregation to overvenerate, the preacher becomes too large in the discussion between God and the people. When this deification occurs, the gospel is impaired.

The gospel is impaired because it is the role of the preacher to design a sermon that cultivates the assurance of grace in core belief. The preacher cultivates the assurance of grace in core belief because the potential power to mend a broken life resides in the core belief of the hearer. Through the presentation of celebrative affirmation (the gospel), the preacher facilitates conversation in core belief between the Holy Spirit and the listener. The Holy Spirit desires, based upon the limitless possibilities in God, to release the hearer's imaginative capacity in core belief. The Holy Spirit releases the imaginative capacity through the remembrance of a redemptive past and/or the conviction of a liberated future, and the hearer attempts to over-record the tapes of fear, hatred, anxiety, etc., with the message of the gospel.

This release of the imaginative capacity (the celebrative moment) becomes empowerment for the hearers to creatively confront their broken lives. Because the limitless possibilities of God are in plain view, people can take personal responsibility for their situation and make the necessary choices to bring their lives in tune with the imaginative possibilities in God. The healing, or the lack thereof, is not in the person and work of the preacher, but in the core belief conversation between God and the hearer. It is not the preacher's responsibility to heal anyone, but to land on a celebrative position, as spokesperson for God, that facilitates conversation between God and the hearer in core belief.[4] Within the core belief conversation of the assurance of grace, hearers experience more confidence in their own capacity to deal with life. Ultimately, the wise preacher is allowing people to take responsibility for their relationship with God, the life, choices, and actions that flow from that relationship.

One distinct stance a preacher can take in sermons to minimize dependency on the preacher and resistance to personal responsibility is the "I" position. Rather than taking the "I" position in preaching, however, the preacher often preaches from the stance of "you." The preacher tells people what they ought to believe and how they ought to behave. The preacher makes statements like "All good Christians come to Bible study." A statement like this has the effect of coercing others to behave in a certain way if they want to be considered "good Christians." It is not that good Christians do not need to come to Bible study; the problem is that in telling people what they ought to believe and how they ought to behave, the preacher runs the risk of ending up stuck with responsibility for their lives. Rather, it is the preacher's task to tell people what and in whom the preacher believes, and to help people discover and accept responsibility for what and in whom they believe.

An illustration of preaching from the "I" position would be a position I took before my congregation. To begin a sermon on the issue of domestic violence and abuse I said:

> After much study, prayer, and reflection, I have come to an important position in regards to abuse and domestic violence. I

do not have to be right, and I know that there are some of you that might disagree with me, but I want to make sure my position is clear. I do not believe that it is God's will for any person to stay in a violent and abusive relationship under the justification that God does not condone divorce. I am not advocating divorce, or an easy exit from the lifelong commitment of marriage, but I believe that God does not desire that anyone subject themselves to abuse and violence. I do not believe that God requires any spouse to be beaten as a part of the marriage covenant. Therefore, if someone is abusive, then the victim of the crime by all means has the right to leave.

In some circles this would be a very controversial declaration, but the emotional envelope the message is delivered in affects the level of resistance the preacher encounters. In other words, the preacher can function in ways to minimize the level of resistance in the hearers. I am not suggesting that we can do away with resistance altogether. Quite to the contrary, resistance is always present, and will get quite intense at times, but the preacher does not have to function in ways that contribute to the resistance. Preaching from the "I" position wraps the message in an emotional envelope that gives people permission to disagree, and this clearly lowers the anxiety in the emotional field. Stating one's position in a way that respects differences lowers the anxiety in the emotional field.

Based upon prayer, study, and reflection, I took a position on God's behalf: I believe God does not require anyone to subject themselves to abuse and violence. The way I presented that position, recognizing and giving full freedom for differences of opinion, allowed people space for clear thinking and praying to discern their own beliefs in the matter. They perceived that there could be the possibility of disagreement with the spokesperson of God without impairing the sustained relationship. When the goal is to make one's own understanding of God's position clear, and not to eradicate differences by speaking for all the people, and all the ages, then it minimizes resistance. It does not do away with resistance by any means, but it minimizes the effect of resistance within the emotional field. It is what the preacher can do to lower anxiety and increase the chance for fresh encounter.

Preaching from the "I" position maximizes the potential that the more mature members of the congregation will feel comfortable about taking an "I" position to agree or disagree with what the preacher said. Parishioners who take personal responsibility for their beliefs will say things like "I disagree with what you said, pastor, on the basis of . . . ," or, "I agree with what you said, on the basis of . . ." The less mature will say things like "No good minister would tell anyone under any circumstances it is appropriate to leave a marriage." These people attempt to eradicate differences by attempting to speak for all the ministers, and all the ages. Some people attempt to coerce preachers into being "good ministers" in the way some ministers attempt to coerce congregants into being "good Christians." Such people focus on the minister to avoid having the responsibility to face the issue, study, pray, and decide for themselves; and such preachers focus on the people and allow overveneration to keep from having to do the same. Preaching from the "I" position avoids the problem of overveneration, and its attendant responsibility for the behavior and salvation of others.

Some will say that preaching from the "I" position is not authoritative enough. They miss the fact that by virtue of the respect and authority as God's spokesperson, the preacher is the principal theologian and shaper of spiritual belief in the congregation. The preacher must demonstrate the maturity to fulfill this rightful position as spiritual head. This maturity is demonstrated by the fact that the preacher can discern a position from God, and feel no need to manipulate, coerce, and cajole people to follow. The preacher has the maturity to hear differences and not sever relationships because of them.

A second stance the preacher can take to minimize the resistance to maturity is to avoid the trap of supplying simplistic answers. As stated earlier, to avoid the ambiguity and fragility of choices in life, some people will deify the preacher and demand certainty. *It is the preacher's task to provide the assurance of grace rather than answers and certainty.* If the preacher would be certain of anything, it must be the assurance of grace.

The preacher's role is well illustrated by a sermon that a young woman in one of my homiletic classes preached on the theme of

"Nothing Shall Separate Us" in the Romans 8:35–39 text. It is diffi-cult to sum up the tremendous depth of an entire sermon in one paragraph, but she said something like this:

> I had a very good and close friend in ministry. My friend was found to be having an affair with someone in the congrega-tion. He decided to go on a weekend retreat in the mountains for a time of renewal and prayer as part of his prescription for healing. He took a gun and killed himself on retreat. . . . My friend believed that there was something, namely his sin, mis-takes, and shortcomings, that could separate him from the love of God. . . . But the text proclaims in Romans 8 that there is nothing in all creation that can separate us from the love of God—neither trouble, hardship, danger, neither angels nor de-mons, neither height nor depth, nor sin of any kind.

My young student did not take a theological position on suicide. She did not judge her friend, his ministry, his behavior, or his life. She was not trying to provide pat answers and certainty, not giving a theological treatise, but offering the assurance of grace that is the gospel.

She offered us so much grace and assurance when she got to the part in the sermon where she said:

> In this world, it was too late for my friend to intimately know this love that cannot separate us from Christ Jesus. But in all of *your* sin, mistakes, and shortcomings, you can intimately know that there is nothing that can separate you from the love of God in Christ Jesus.

She gave us the assurance that God's grace was available through all of *our* personal trials and hardships. She taught and instructed us, lifted and inspired us, and most of all gave us the hope of the gospel. She gave us the best sermon that she, or any preacher, can give: she put us in touch with the God behind the text who has unlimited means to assure us of grace. In the final analysis, the best chance that we have to minimize resistance is to offer the assurance of grace.

The first two sections of this chapter have suggested that the preacher who would design for celebration must prepare the emo-tional context by giving attention to the organizing principles of a

celebrative sermon and cultivate a relational presence that will minimize resistance. We must also prepare the content that is to be placed
within the emotional context. We now turn to the preparation of
content.

SERMON PREPARATION FROM AN EXPERIENTIAL ORIENTATION

Before outlining the actual process of generating the content of the
celebrative sermon, we must discuss three critical assumptions. First,
if we are going to develop content for a sermon that celebrates, we
must have an experientially oriented preparation process. Experiential orientation in preparation means that we prepare the sermon
from the cognitive, emotive, and intuitive aspects of human awareness. In the traditional sermonic preparation process, too much emphasis has been placed on the cognitive, which leads to an overvalu-
ation placed on exegesis and rational inquiry. This is not to say that
exegesis and rational inquiry are not critically important. Exegesis
and rational inquiry are absolutely essential to quality preaching, but
when exegesis is opened to include the emotive and intuitive, the
preacher is able to generate images that shape and order experience.
The effect of this is that the preacher comes off not as a distant
scholar but as an eyewitness who has *experienced* the text-event and
invites others to experience the same. Exegesis that includes the
emotive and intuitive allows preachers to shape truth gleaned from
rigorous scholarship into images that have deep interiority. If we
would develop content for a celebrative sermon, we must design an
experientially oriented preparation process that includes the whole
person.

Second, we must acknowledge that one of the critical advantages
of an experientially oriented preparation process is that the preacher
is placed within a framework to experience the sermon in preparation. The goal of the celebrative sermon is for people to experience
the assurance of grace, and if the people are going to experience the
sermon in delivery, then the preacher must experience it in preparation. If the preacher does not experience anything in preparation,
then, with great certainty, we can predict that the people will not

experience anything in delivery. The experiential nature of the sermon for the congregation begins with the preacher, and the experiential nature of the preacher's preparation.

The third assumption revolves around the resolution of a critical
question that many ask as they approach content preparation: which
comes first, the biblical text or the sermon idea? Some homileticians
believe that the biblical text must come first, and then the sermon
idea; others reverse the order. The approach of celebrative design is
to begin preparation with whichever comes first in the preacher's
thinking, because experientially oriented sermons only happen at
the intersection of the streets of life and the biblical text. If you are
travelling north on the street of life, and God stops you with a sermon idea, take the idea and keep traveling north until you intersect
the street of the biblical text. If you are traveling east on the street of
biblical text (i.e., the lectionary), and God stops you with a text, take
it, and keep traveling east until you intersect the street of life. *Sermons
that order and shape experience only happen at the intersection of the streets
of life and the biblical text.* In celebrative design, there is not much
discussion about which comes first, text or sermonic idea, because
the experiential sermon only happens at this crucial intersection,
and it makes little difference which road one is traveling on to get
there.

Assuming that we have a biblical text or a sermon idea, let us now
define a content preparation process that would yield a celebrative
sermon. The experiential preparation process that begets celebration
would include prayer, free association, homiletical exegesis, the preaching worksheet, and the written drafts.

Prayer

Fundamental to the preparation of any celebrative sermon is prayer.
When we infuse preparation with prayer, we assume God is interested in the preaching process. If God is interested in the preaching
process, then we are not left to human devices and purposes alone—
we have a help, an aid, a comforter, a creative catalyst, an encourager,
and a guide. The Holy Spirit goes along beside us in the journey
from preparation to actual delivery of the sermon. Any preacher who

would ignore this help offered through the vehicle of prayer has no understanding of the awesome task that is before the preacher.

Many of us realize that we need the help of the Holy Spirit, but we do not get the Spirit "on board" until just before the point of delivery, often as we are standing before the people. If this is the only, or the most fervent, place the preacher has invited God to be involved, then usually it is too late, though God does sometimes tend to be merciful. If we want the Spirit to truly help and guide, then that help and guidance must come from the very beginning. If the Holy Spirit is going to do transformative work in the lives of people, the Spirit must be involved at the point where we commence sermon preparation.

Involving the Spirit from the very beginning through prayer allows us to get in contact with God's intention for the sermon. In preparing the sermon, it is important to synchronize our intention with that of God. The preacher might ask in prayer:

> God, how do you want the gospel to help your people to grow this week? What is the most appropriate text to help them grow? What are the real needs in the fellowship/world that this biblical text or sermon idea could address? God, how is it that you desire to speak to your people?

Prayer places us in the posture to discern what God wants to accomplish in the midst of the gathered congregation. God's intention for the sermon can only be accessed through disciplined and fervent prayer.

Free Association

Following prayer, the process of free association upon the sermon idea or biblical text allows the emotive and intuitive aspects of human awareness to become fully engaged in the preparation process. Traditionally, the preacher would go directly from prayer to exegesis, and often this movement either locks the emotive and intuitive out of the process, or the emotive and intuitive is not consulted until the writing stage. Adding the emotive and intuitive so late in the process guarantees that the sermon will be dominated by the cognitive. Therefore, it is important that free association happen early, so that it can be a full partner in the preparation process. When we allow free association full partnership, the emotive and intuitive will supply vital images and energy that are so critically necessary if the sermon is to be an experiential encounter.

The methodology for free association is to write either the biblical text or the sermon idea in the center of a blank sheet of paper and allow whatever thoughts, feelings, images, or ideas that come to mind to be recorded. We do mean *free* association, so whatever comes to mind is fair game. Many times one discovers and records some very interesting and unexpected data: maybe a person you have not thought of in fifteen years, or a vivid experience that happened to you just last week, or a story that you have heard told a thousand times; or maybe a song or hymn, a person, a prayer, connecting Bible verses, or maybe your first date comes to mind. Also, the tragic and painful experiences come to mind: the funeral of one of your loved ones, the feeling you had as they closed your eyes for surgery, the numbness that came to your body when you heard the word "cancer." Any and all information that is thrown to the surface of our minds is appropriate to be placed upon the sheet.

The result of this free association is that if we allow ourselves enough time and patience, the data on the page will take some shape or form. If we permit ourselves to stay with the process, we might discover that a pattern is recorded on the page, and at least some of the recorded information forms a whole. The page represents what the emotive and the intuitive send forth in response to the stimuli of the biblical text/sermonic idea. Usually it is not until we are working on the Preaching Worksheet, or the actual writing of the sermon that the pattern is clear enough to decide what material to include or drop. Every piece of material on the free association sheet is a candidate for inclusion as an opening story, illustration, poem, closing celebration, etc., in this sermon or, if we maintain a filing system, in some future sermon. People often wonder how good preachers find just the right story or illustration to fit perfectly with and in the sermon. The process of free association that we have outlined will draw forth emotive and intuitive material that, if handled properly, will fit the sermon "like a glove."[5]

Unencumbered and meditative free association will usually produce powerful insights and materials, plus fascinating illustrations, texts, sermon ideas, stories, pictures, jokes, scholarly material, songs, poems, quotes, experiences, names, places, dates, faces, etc. The combination of prayer and free association will usually yield powerful personal and communal experiences of the biblical text and life. Prayer and free association set the stage for the next step in the content preparation process, homiletical exegesis.

Homiletical Exegesis

Assuming we have engaged prayer and free association, and that we have the text, exegesis now comes to center stage. When we suggest exegesis, we mean exegesis from the perspective of African American homiletics and hermeneutics, or what celebrative design calls *homiletical exegesis.* The central question for African American homiletical exegesis is: what *meaning* (assurance) does the gospel shed on the human condition of suffering through the particular biblical text to be preached? The search for meaning has to do with the existential human condition that Viktor E. Frankl describes when he says: "to live is to suffer, to survive is to find meaning in the suffering."[6] Homiletical exegesis believes that the gospel overcomes all suffering and therefore supplies *meaning* to every experience of tragedy, suffering, evil, and death.

Homiletical exegesis discerns meaning in the text through two primary steps: (1) traditional exegesis, which attempts to ascertain what the author of the passage meant to communicate, and (2) experiential hermeneutics, which relates the exegetical message to the existential condition of human suffering.[7] Homiletical exegesis brings these two steps together to discover God's meaning in the biblical passage, and therefore the assurance of grace to be shared in the sermon.

Traditional exegesis involves discovering, as accurately as possible, what the biblical author intended to communicate in the composing and writing of the text. The traditional exegete asks this pivotal question: when the original listeners heard/read the text, what did *they* understand the author to mean? In other words, if I were a member of the Corinthian church when Paul's first letter arrived, what message would I receive? Traditional exegesis attempts to interpret the text from the vantage point of sitting in a seat in the Corinthian church, and/or sitting with Paul in his study or cell as he composes his thoughts for Corinth. To gain this vantage point, we apply all the critical skills of the exegetical process: historical-grammatical method, rhetorical and literary analysis, original languages, etc. Our main purpose is to comprehend the message of the text as if we were one of the persons to whom it was written.

Many exegetes stop at the point of discovering what message the author intended to convey when the text was written, find points of application for our time, and begin writing the sermon. But there is another critically important step in homiletical exegesis, and that is to ask the question of meaning: How does the message of the text give assurance of grace to the existential human condition of suffering? In other words, what good news does this text bring to the experiential suffering, tragedy, and evil in the world? These questions move exegesis beyond intellectual and philosophical sources to ground it in the actual life and experience of people.

It took several years of pastoral experience for me to integrate traditional exegesis with life, that is, to integrate exegesis with the profound human search for meaning and hope. There was a pastoral encounter that crystallized the integration, and signaled my intentional movement to homiletical exegesis. One of the members of the congregation was dying of cancer. She called me from the hospital in the latter stages of her battle and emphatically asked me to come to her bedside. At the time she called, I was preparing a sermon, and doing exegesis on the text in John 11:25–26:

> Jesus said to her, "I am the resurrection and the life. Those who believe in me, even though they die, will live, and everyone who lives and believes in me will never die. Do you believe this?"

I immediately went to see her. When I got to her hospital room, she had an agenda, and expressed the desire that her pastor read the Twenty-third Psalm to her for comfort and strength. I read the psalm, but when I looked at her, there was a searching in her eyes. It was very close to the end now. She knew it, and I knew it. Her eyes asked me for a word of hope that might help her face the situation. She looked deep into my eyes to my soul, and when I looked there, I encountered the text of John 11:25-26. I remembered that in my exegetical work there was discussion of whether these were the very words of Jesus. Some believed that Jesus might not have uttered these words, and that they might be a gloss, a redaction on the text. Could I utter to this woman in tremendous need a possible redaction on the text?

At that point, I made the decision that what the commentator said was important to consider, but not of ultimate concern. This woman was facing her own death and looking for meaning, assurance, and hope. In light of her concrete situation, the discussion about a possible redaction on the text seemed to pale in significance. The question was one of meaning and assurance: did I (she) *believe* the text? Did I (she) *believe* that even though death was imminent, Jesus could give life beyond death? I believed the text[8] and read to her:

> Jesus said to her, "I am the resurrection and the life. Those who believe in me, even though they die, will live, and everyone who lives and believes in me will never die. Do you believe this?"

I was pointed, direct, and compassionate when I asked her from within the text, "Do you believe this?" The gospel was offering an assurance of grace, and the question was, did she believe it? When we deal with matters of life and death, we are in the realm of intuitive core belief, and what tapes of trust one has established. The gospel was available to over-record tapes of fear, and/or strengthen tapes of trust, but that could only happen as she honestly responded to the question of whether or not she believed. As much as I compassionately cared for her, I could not answer that question for her. I could only offer the assurance of grace to address her life and death. We will return to this, but homiletical exegesis is the process of *mining* the celebrative and affirmative truth of the gospel to offer meaning and hope to the experience of suffering, tragedy, evil, and death.

I suggested that it took me several years to integrate traditional exegesis with life, because it took time to realize that it is possible to discover the historical sources of the text, and not grasp meaning. It took time and experience to realize that exegesis could be used to secure important information, i.e., the form, the literary style, redaction, etc., and yet the exegete still might *miss* meaning and ultimate concern in the text. The function of exegetical tools is not to discover sources in and of themselves, but source information to help the preacher discover meaning. The process of traditional exegesis to discover what the author intended to communicate is the first step in discovering what *meaning* the Holy Spirit intended in the text.

I do not mean to imply that homiletical exegesis is an easy process. This is why I used the word *mine* several paragraphs back. The preacher must mine, unearth, dig up, excavate, and extract meaning (good news) to address human life. The words *mine, excavate,* etc., are carefully chosen to describe a process of struggle, whereby the preacher goes deep under the surface of the human heart, and deep under the surface of the biblical text to offer meaning and hope. This is a difficult process because human beings seem to have a knack for easily interpreting and expressing bad news. Many people are experts at bad news, but novices at interpreting and expressing meaning and hope. The preacher must not be a novice at good news because though the good news is readily available in the biblical text, the preacher must be willing to move past clichés and pat answers, put a hard hat on, get down in the mud and mire of human life, survey the multifaceted terrain of the gospel text, and extract nuggets of gospel truth and assurance.

My experience has been that gospel truth is not always on the surface of the text and the veneer of life. The preacher has to labor, sweat, struggle, study, pray, wrestle with the text, tussle with life, grapple with self, and sometimes scuffle with God to discover God's meaning. Preaching the assurance of grace to suffering, tragedy, evil, and death is one of the most agonizing yet most exhilarating experiences in life. Often, the exhilaration is in direct proportion to the scuffle, strain, and toil. I do not know how some have come to expect that preaching the assurance of grace is an easy and casual task. Though we have the Holy Spirit as an aid, comforter, catalyst, etc., and the biblical record is sure ground for celebration, preaching the assurance of grace is one of the most difficult things in my life.

Most homiletic methods spend much time on interpreting the text, and *some* spend time on examining life and the community, but *few* spend time exploring the preacher's self and the preacher's core belief.[9] Not allowing a text to address the preacher's own core belief impairs the discovery of meaning. It is a struggle of the highest order in my life to truly allow the text to encounter me in my inner core. In some sense, it is only after I have been encountered by the text that I can offer an experience of encounter (experiential encounter) to hearers.

Practically, it is not possible for any preacher to discover meaning in *every* text, because sometimes we do not have the eyes and ears of life and experience to encounter the text. But on the other hand, there are some texts that could be preached, but are not, because the exegetical approach of the preacher limits perception. Perception of meaning is limited if traditional exegesis separates sources from existential suffering, tragedy, and evil. When this occurs, the preacher is informed, but is not sure what to do with the information. The preacher has exegetics, but cannot ground it in the experience of people, and therefore does not have meaning. The preacher with exegetical information must ask the question of meaning: what assurance is contained in this exegetical information that will address suffering, tragedy, and the life and death concerns of people? I believe every text in the Bible is grounded in some human experiential need that the text seeks to address and resolve. The preacher who would divorce exegetics from the experiential need the text seeks to address is peddling information and ignoring experience.

To preach a text, and not share with congregants one's view of its meaning, is to place oneself in serious jeopardy with the hearers. I made this cardinal mistake when I preached a sermon on the text of 1 Corinthians 14:34, where Paul advises women to be silent in church. I listed five exegetical options to the meaning of this text, and concluded the sermon by telling the congregation to make what choice of interpretation they desired. My phone jumped off the hook with irate congregants, who appreciated the options but wanted to know which one the pastor believed. (*Remember! The preacher has the responsibility to land on a celebrative position that facilitates conversation between the people and God.*) I was the resident theologian, and they wanted to know what I believed. What I believed had to do with the meaning

I discerned from the exegetical options in the text, experiences in life, and my core belief. I had the responsibility to share what I believed was the meaning in the text.

Exegetical information without meaning leaves hearers participating in an intellectual exercise, but not encountering the text. Therefore, to help people encounter the text, the preacher should not preach any text that the preacher does not deeply believe. Hearers do not come to church to hear the preacher's doubts, they have enough of their own already. If the preacher does not deeply believe a text, then the text is not ready for preaching. There is nothing wrong with acknowledging that one is not ready to preach a text as a result of a question about meaning and belief. What is much more problematic is to decline to preach a text based upon the fact that one's exegetical approach to the text limits perception.

As an example of the process of homiletical exegesis, I would like to look at the treatment of the text in Colossians 1:16–17:

> For by him all things in heaven and on earth were created, things visible and invisible, whether thrones or dominions or rulers or powers—all things were created by him and for him. He himself is before all things, and in him all things hold together.

To preach this text effectively requires a fair amount of exegesis, and therefore it has great potential to be preached as intellectual doctrine, cognitive abstraction, and philosophical theology. The key is to discern human concern and existential need underneath the text by placing exegesis in dialogue with tragedy, suffering, evil, and death.

Applying traditional exegetical method, I found out that the proto-Gnostics in the Colossians text took a position on the question of evil. They decided that evil was perpetrated by "aeons," "emanations" (powers, principalities, etc., for Paul), projected out of the being of God, that negatively influenced human activity. These powers had to be appeased to gain favor in human affairs. The Pauline response to the heresy was to stress the eternal significance of Christ as Sovereign over everything in heaven and earth, visible and invisible. Because Christ created everything, everything was subject to Christ, even the powers. The Christian had no need to placate any powers because Christ was Sovereign of all. Paul encountered the heresy by exalting the central role of Christ in the cosmic order and by asserting that Christ was in charge and control of the whole universe.

In applying the second step of homiletical exegesis I asked this question: How does Paul's message impact the existential concern of suffering, tragedy, evil, and death? Human beings, regardless of race, nationality, or culture, experience evil, and have the desire to come to terms with it, define its place in the cosmic order, and have assurance of victory over evil. The need for assurance of victory over evil was sought by the Pauline generation, and is sought by every generation that has ever lived, including ours. Paul offered the assurance of grace to this existential concern of evil by establishing that Christ is the creator of all things, and in him all things hold together. Therefore, the Christian need not placate any powers, visible, or invisible, because in Christ all evil is overcome. This is the meaning of this text that gives us the assurance of grace in the face of any suffering, tragedy, or evil. The preacher need only identify with the suffering of the people, and allow this meaning to address the concrete situations and circumstances experienced by the hearers.

Sometimes after all the strain and toil for the assurance of grace, it will come down to the simple matter of whether or not one can trust God. Sometimes there is no understanding of an experience that will render meaning, or the quest for meaning takes extended time. In these circumstances, there is only the assurance that comes from trusting God. A popular African American hymn by W. B. Stevens expresses this sentiment when the writer says:

Farther along we'll know all about it,
Farther along we'll understand why;
Cheer up, my brother, live in the sunshine,
We'll understand it all by and by.[10]

The song deeply expresses the thought and feeling that in regard to some experiences in life, we must simply trust God. Some things are desperately tragic, and we will not understand, or cannot explain, but farther along we will know all about it. The song recognizes that sometimes the quest for meaning takes time, but if we trust God, meaning and hope will come. Because we trust God, and can trust our lives to God, in the face of grievous adversity we can cheer up and live in the sunshine. It is an amazing assurance of grace to simply trust God.

The preacher must, through the process of homiletical exegesis, determine the meaning the Holy Spirit intends to communicate. Only upon discerning the Spirit's meaning in the text are we ready to begin the Preaching Worksheet.

The Preaching Worksheet

After continual prayer, free association, and homiletical exegesis to discern meaning, we are ready to prepare the Preaching Worksheet. The Preaching Worksheet is designed to help the preacher synthesize all the information, experience, and meaning gathered to this point in the various steps of preparation. The result of this synthesis is that the preacher is helped to intentionally shape the purpose, suspense, resolution, and celebration of the celebrative sermon. This intentional shaping is accomplished by decisive responses to every question of the Preaching Worksheet. The preacher moves deliberately to respond decisively to each question until the preacher reaches the two most critical sections of the Preaching Worksheet: the Behavioral Purpose Statement (Question 5), and the Strategy for Celebration (Questions 6a, 6b, and 6c).

The Behavioral Purpose Statement is critical because it forces the preacher to state specifically the way in which the sermon is to influence the behavior of the listener. No preacher can totally predict the behavioral result of any sermon, but the Holy Spirit can encounter the listener in a fresh and dynamic way if the preacher prayerfully targets a behavioral result, and then carefully focuses the sermon toward that result. The more deliberately focused the preacher is about targeting a behavioral result, the better able the Holy Spirit is to invite the listener to respond to the sermon's challenge for behavioral change.

The Behavioral Purpose Statement (Question 5) is divided into two clauses:

(1) I propose to _____

(2) to the end hearers will_____ .

The Preaching Worksheet

1. What does this passage say to me?

2. What does this passage say to the needs of people in our time?

3. What is the "bad news" in the text? What is the "bad news" for our time?

4. What is the "good news" in the text? What is the "good news" for our time?

5. *Behavioral Purpose Statement*

I propose _____

to the end hearers will _____ .

6. *Strategy for Celebration*

a. What shall we celebrate?
b. How shall we celebrate our response to 6a?
c. What materials of celebration shall we use?

Many preachers are able to quickly and readily respond to the cognitive aspects of the first clause. For example, based upon the text of 1 Samuel 14:15, 23 one might complete this first clause: *I propose to show, through a case study of Israel's battle with the Philistines, the critical need in the African American community for blacksmiths.* What is most difficult is to target influence on behavior, and decide what we would want people to do or become after we demonstrate the first clause. The preacher must continually ask the questions: "After hearing the sermon, what do we want people to do or become?" or "If I accomplish the first clause, then so what? What difference will it make in the lives of people?" Many sermons are unclear about the second behavioral clause, and therefore leave people with few concrete directions, or little real spiritual empowerment.

The full Behavioral Purpose Statement for 1 Samuel 14:15, 23 might look like this:

> I propose to show, through a case study of Israel's battle with the Philistines, the critical need in the African American community for blacksmiths, to the end that hearers will choose trades as a means through which God will deliver the community from its problems and despair.[11]

The Behavioral Purpose Statement targets influence on behavior as the fundamental goal of the sermon, and not an appendage that is attended to with a few points of "application." The goal of the sermon is to influence behavior, to encourage hearers to consider how God might use trades to deliver the community.

Some homileticians shrink from this concrete emphasis on behavioral change, seeming to prefer propositional preaching or what Charles Jefferson calls "academic" preaching. Jefferson says:

> There are two kinds of preaching. There is what we may call "Academic" preaching, the unfolding of ideas and truths for the sake of the ideas and truths themselves. . . . It is always interesting work to take an idea or principle and give an exposition of it, unfolding its beauty, exploring its meaning. Many rejoice in that sort of intellectual work, and many other people greatly enjoy seeing them do it. . . . On the other hand there is "Practical" preaching. . . . I am not interested in abstractions in the pulpit. In my library at home, with books of philosophy around me, I can have a good time in the realm of theory and speculation, but as soon as I get into the pulpit, I am always practical. . . . *I care nothing for the unfolding of ideas unless I can apply them to the conduct of individuals and institutions.*[12]

As a proponent of behavioral purpose, I prefer, in Jefferson's terms, practical preaching, and believe that preaching must be practical if it is going to be effective. But I go even further than this and question the artificial split between "Practical" and "Academic" preaching. If we look closely at the Bible, we discover that the biblical text never merely informs. The Bible rarely, if ever, "unfolds ideas and truths for the sake of ideas themselves." All texts in the Bible have the intention to influence, and often outright change, behavior. As Jefferson suggests, at home in our libraries or with our theological friends we might have fun with speculation, information, and abstraction, but in the pulpit, the preacher must influence behavior.

Without question, the production of the Behavioral Purpose Statement is the most difficult part of the Preaching Worksheet. No preacher is ready to write or preach the sermon until there is a pulsating, vibrant statement of purpose. H. Grady Davis supports this contention by quoting John Henry Jowett:

> No sermon is ready for preaching, nor writing out, until we can express its theme in a short, pregnant sentence as clear as a crystal. I find the getting of that sentence the hardest, the most exacting, and the most fruitful labor in my study. To compel oneself to fashion that sentence, to dismiss every word that is vague, ragged, ambiguous, to think oneself through to a form of words which defines the theme with scrupulous exactness—this is surely one of the most vital and essential factors in the making of a sermon: and I do not think any sermon ought to be preached or even written, until that sentence has emerged, clear and lucid as a cloudless moon.[13]

As difficult as it might be to achieve, the Behavioral Purpose Statement must be "clear and lucid as a cloudless moon," because it serves as the flight plan for the sermonic experience. If the flight plan is unclear, then it follows that the pilot (preacher) is probably unclear about where the plane (sermon) is going, and unclear about when and where the passengers (listeners) will arrive. Just as the pilot cannot leave the terminal without a filed flight plan, no sermon is ready to be written or preached until a clear and lucid Behavioral Purpose Statement is filed with the Holy Spirit.

The second critical section of the Preaching Worksheet is the Strategy for Celebration, in which the preacher gives attention to the final stage of the sermon and how the preacher will close through celebration. The importance of the closing stage of celebration to African American preaching is witnessed in the fact that the luminary preacher Martin Luther King Jr., in a conversation about the first steps of sermon preparation, said, "The first thing I think about is how I am going to close."[14] According to Wyatt T. Walker, the first thing King considered in preparation was the strategy for celebration. The Strategy for Celebration is the thoughtful, intentional, and deliberate shaping of the celebration that culminates the celebrative sermon.

Some expect that celebration is spontaneous, unplanned, and a response to the moment, but experience teaches that the more the preacher shapes the celebration in advance, the more celebrative spontaneity can occur in delivery. To maximize the possibility that the sermon will shift and transform perspective, attitude, feeling, and commitment through celebration, the preacher must carefully plan the celebration/assurance of grace.

The preacher shapes the Strategy for Celebration by decisive responses to the three-part Question 6 of the Preaching Worksheet:

a. *What shall we celebrate?*

b. *How shall we celebrate our response in 6a?*

c. *What materials of celebration shall we use?*

The Preaching Worksheet is designed so that a decisive response to each question is predicated upon a decisive response to a previous question. Question 6a—What shall we celebrate?—is predicated on a decisive response to Question 4—What is the "good news" in the text? What is the "good news" for our time? One of the cardinal rules of the Preaching Worksheet is that the preacher always and only celebrates the good news. Celebration is grounded in the good news of the text, and it is that good news that is lifted, exalted, and joyfully reinforced. Let's look at the Preaching Worksheet for 1 Samuel 14:15, 23 starting with Question 4, and complete the entire Question 6:

4. *What is the "good news" in the text? What is the "good news" for our time?* God used the faith, weapon, and ingenuity of Jonathan to give Israel the victory in the battle, on the way to giving them victory in the war with the Philistines. While Israel was in fear, and complaining about the lack of smiths and few weapons, God used what weapons they did have to win victory. God is never defeated, and always will help God's people, when we have faith in God and use what resources we do have in the community.

6. *Strategy for Celebration*

a. *What shall we celebrate?* We shall celebrate the providence and power of God that is never defeated when God's people battle the enemy with the resources of the community, coupled with faith in God.

b. *How shall we celebrate our response in 6a?* The sermon will be structured such that the complication of the text, the lack of smiths and weapons in the army, is resolved in the faith, creativity, and ingenuity of Jonathan, whom God used to win a battle.

c. *What materials of celebration shall we use?* In response to the faith and ingenuity of Jonathan, God sent an earthquake to win the battle. All God needs is one.

Question 4 forces the preacher to discover what is the good news (meaning) in the text, and Question 6a helps the preacher intentionally and specifically plan to celebrate that good news in the sermon.

Questions 4 and 6a, as well as most of the other questions on the Preaching Worksheet, are *what* questions, and *what* questions tend to foster content. Question 6b is a *how* question, and *how* questions tend to operate at the level of emotional process. Question 6b asks, *how* shall we celebrate the *what* of 6a? Practically and concretely, how will we structure the sermon so that the *what* of 6a (the content) is delivered at the right moment with the right sense of timing?

In the Preaching Worksheet of 1 Samuel 14:15, 23, the response to Question 6b suggests that the sermon is structured in the intuitive form of situation-complication-resolution-celebration, and the victory of Jonathan resolves the complication of few weapons and smiths. The preacher manages the emotional process of the sermon by clearly and experientially setting forth the situation and complication, then the good news is supplied to resolve the complication, and the sermon moves up to celebration. This management of emotional process gives increased eloquence and intensity to the content of the good news found in Question 6a.

Question 6c asks about the materials we will use to celebrate. Much more will be said about the materials of celebration in the next chapter, but materials of celebration could be the use of stories, scripture, music, poems, etc., to joyfully and ecstatically reinforce the good news of the sermon.

The Written Drafts

Upon the completion of the Preaching Worksheet, the preacher is ready to begin writing the sermon. It is important to note that the sermon should go through several written drafts before actual delivery. Experience teaches that writing sharpens sermonic focus, and allows careful attention to the movement and unity that are critical to any quality sermon. The more drafts of the sermon the preacher can edit, in all probability the clearer the preacher is in the presentation of the sermon: *clear and precise writing that develops clarity of thought is indispensable to clear and precise preaching*[15] Careful editing of several drafts helps the preacher to experience the sermonic system as a whole and therefore gain clues as to what the listeners might experience. Since what the preacher experiences in preparation is probably what the people will experience in delivery, review and revision of several drafts will help to ensure that the sermon is indeed a celebrative experiential encounter.

With all the information and experience of preparation synthesized on the Preaching Worksheet, the place to begin the writing process is to focus upon the Behavioral Purpose Statement (Question 5). As the controlling purpose that regulates every aspect of the sermon, the Behavioral Purpose serves as the gate for what materials of exegesis, free association, and celebration find entrance into the sermon. The preacher only allows the stories, poems, illustrations, exegesis, etc. (content), that serve to accomplish the Behavioral Purpose. With the Behavioral Purpose clear and in view, the preacher can then turn to the Strategy for Celebration (Question 6) for clues to structure, emotional process, and celebration that manage the content of the sermon. A focus on the Behavioral Purpose and the Strategy for Celebration sets the stage for the inclusion of the imaginative capacity.

What occurs in the writing process can be difficult to describe, but if the preacher has prayerfully and thoroughly followed through in the various stages of the preparation process, then creativity within the imagination is unleashed. As the imaginative capacity is released, the preparation of content and of emotional context come together to give creative and celebrative insight. As the preacher labors with the writing process, the preacher is in the very heart of the sermon, where creativity, ingenuity, inventiveness, and, most of all, the Holy Spirit shape and direct toward the celebrative encounter. Through the lenses of the imaginative capacity, the preacher consults the Preaching Worksheet over and over again, chiseling and hammering words, thoughts, feelings, and ideas until it is clear what to say and how to say it.

Sometimes creativity and imagination do not flow in one session or one draft, and the sermon needs incubation time, where the preacher has to get away from the process for a while. Sometimes, while the preacher is doing something else completely away from the writing process, at another level preparation is still going on, and suddenly—flash!—some insight comes that brings the whole sermon together. The insight came from somewhere deep within the imaginative capacity, helped by the preacher's preparation and the graciousness of the Holy Spirit.

The preacher's goal is to involve the imaginative capacity in much the way James Weldon Johnson describes in the creation of the African American classic "Lift Every Voice and Sing."[16] Johnson says:

> I talked it over with my brother . . . and we planned to write a song . . . to have it sung by schoolchildren—a chorus of five hundred voices. I got my first line: Lift ev'ry voice and sing. Not a startling line, but I worked along grinding out the next five. When, near the end of the first stanza, there came to me the lines:
>
>> Sing a song full of the faith that the dark past has taught us.
>> Sing a song full of the hope that the present has brought us.
>
> The spirit of the poem had taken hold of me. . . . In composing the two other stanzas, I did not need pen and paper. As I worked through the opening and middle lines of the last stanza:

God of our weary years
God of our silent tears,
Thou who has brought us thus far on the way
Thou who has by thy might
Led us into the light
Keep us forever in the path we pray; . . .

I could not keep back the tears, and made no effort to do so. I
was experiencing the transports of the poet's ecstasy. Feverish
ecstasy was followed by contentment—that sense of serene joy—
which makes artistic creation the most complete of all human
experiences. . . . The only comment we can make is we wrote
better than we knew.[17]

The preacher seeks to release this imaginative capacity in the writing process of the sermon such that it can be said, "The preacher
preached better than he/she knew." We do not want to set the expectation that this process will occur every week during preparation,
but the goal is for it to occur as often as possible. Every week we
preachers aim for this goal, whether or not we reach it. The closer
the preacher is to "contentment—that sense of serene joy—which
makes artistic creation the most complete of all human experiences,"
the more ready the sermon is for delivery to the people.

The author was helped to understand the value of writing to quality
and effective preaching upon reading *A Writer's Time: A Guide to the
Creative Process, from Vision through Revision*.[18] Though the book is
written from the perspective of helping people write to publish, the
insights about persuasive and effective writing, and the setting forth
of methodology that leads to persuasive and effective writing, are an
invaluable and immediate help for any preacher who desires to preach
well. In the future, homileticians must give much more attention to
the discipline of writing to help increase the effectiveness of sermons.

This is a very good place to address the often discussed question
of whether it is better to use a manuscript, outline, or neither during
the delivery of the sermon. Preachers are different; for some, outlines
facilitate confidence, for others the manuscript facilitates ease of delivery, and still others seem to need neither manuscript nor outline as

they extemporaneously develop the sermon before the people. Preachers should use whatever method facilitates confidence and ease of delivery, but the basis of any sermon delivered to the people should be several clearly written and edited drafts of the sermon. For preachers who use manuscripts, it is obvious that the written draft is the basis of delivery. In discussion with the best preachers that use only an outline, and the best preachers who seem extemporaneous, they both talk of several written drafts in the study that the people rarely see. Once clarity of thought and design occurs through the process of several written drafts, the choice of delivery form is whatever facilitates confidence and ease of delivery for the preacher.

Earlier in this chapter, we said that celebration/assurance of grace was the goal of the sermon, and the final stage of the sermon through which the goal is achieved. This final stage is so decisive to the celebrative sermon that we will look at it critically in the next chapter, "Guidelines for Celebration."

5

Guidelines for Celebration

In the previous chapter we established that celebration is the culmination of the sermonic design, where, by application of the
gospel to the complications of life, a moment is created in which
the remembrance of a redemptive past and/or the conviction of a
liberated future transforms the present reality of the listener. Celebration is both *the goal* of the emotional process of the sermon
and *the final stage* of the sermon through which the goal culminates and is achieved. The goal of celebration and celebrative emotional process is severely hobbled by an ineffective and inadequate
closing in this final stage. Therefore, this chapter will set forth
guidelines that will help the preacher increase effectiveness in closing the sermon. We begin with a discussion of celebration as *ecstatic reinforcement*.

CELEBRATION AS ECSTATIC REINFORCEMENT

The roots of the theory of celebration in the final stage are in the
tradition of African American folk preaching that has always concluded the sermon with what could be called "climactic utterance." A classic example is the closing stage of the sermon preached
by Uncle Pompey in "Uncle Wash's Funeral." Uncle Pompey brings
the sermon to the final stage of climactic utterance when he says:

> Then he went to talkin' 'bout a vision of Jacob's ladder. "I
> see Jacob's ladder. An' I see Brother Wash. He's climbin' Jacob's
> ladder. Look like he's half way up. I want y'all to pray with
> me that he enter the pearly gates, Brothers and Sisters. He's
> still a climbin'. I see the pearly gates. They is swingin' open.

An' I see Brother Wash. He has done reached the topmost round of de ladder. Let us sing with all our hearts that blessed hymn, "There Is a Fountain Filled with Blood."

When they sang the second verse, 'bout the dyin' thief rejoiced to see that fountain in his day, Uncle Pompey cried out over the crowd, "I see Brother Wash as he enters in, an' that dyin' thief is there to welcome him in. Thank God! Thank God! He's made it into Paradise. His sins has been washed away, an' he has landed safe forever more."

Well sir, I don't need to tell you that the women started to shout on the first verse, an' when they got to singin' 'bout the dyin' thief in heaven, an' they seen the 'surance of grace that was in it, they like to never quit praisin' God.

Henry H. Mitchell labeled this tradition of climactic utterance celebration, and lifted it up as the genius of African American preaching.[1] From the perspective of homiletic method, Mitchell provided an excellent interpretive foundation upon which to build and expand.

Celebration in the final stage of the sermon functions as *the joyful and ecstatic reinforcement of the truth already taught and delivered in the main body of the sermon.* It is a commonplace expectation that a composer crafts the emotional process of a symphony to conclude with a distinctive ending that heightens and enhances the experience of the music to reinforce meaning deep within the being of the hearer. The preacher handles emotional process in a similar manner, concluding the sermon with climactic utterance that heightens and enhances the experience of the sermon. Lifting up the good news of the sermon, the preacher joyfully and ecstatically celebrates it to reinforce meaning in core belief.

Uncle Pompey, through heightened imagery, metaphor, rhetoric, and imagination in the final stage of celebration, ecstatically reinforced the good news of the gospel that was delivered in the main body of the sermon. The good news of the gospel was that being arrested and convicted on earth did not keep one out of heaven. Uncle Pompey ecstatically bolstered the good news until it intensified in core belief, and with the help of the Holy Spirit, the people experienced a shift in perspective, attitude, feeling, and commitment. Through the dynamics of the assurance of grace, the hearers experienced a transformation of grief and loss, and as Ned Walker says, "they like to never quit praisin' God."

To mention celebration and emotion in the climaxing of sermons stirs fear of manipulation and abuse in some. Rather than risking abuse or overuse of emotion, many have either attempted to throw emotion out altogether or have severely curtailed its use and expression in the sermonic process. This is an example of the proverbial "throwing the baby out with the bath water." We must not miss the critical fact that celebrative emotions are a natural and inherent part of the gospel. As we outlined with the example of Mary Magdalene in chapter 2, whenever the gospel is received and personally appropriated in core belief, celebrative emotions such as praise and thanksgiving are part of the intuitive experience and response. There are celebrative emotions that are inherently part of the gospel, and to deny these emotions is to reject a significant component of the emotional process that ushers in the transformative power of the gospel. The gospel will never reach intuitive core belief without the full participation of emotion in the emotional process.

When we curtail the use and expression of emotion in the sermonic process, we ignore the critical insight that sermons have an emotive logic as well as a cognitive logic, and both are equally important in preaching a celebrative sermon. Mitchell states:

> The logic of emotive consciousness is as important and coherent as the logic of human reason. Human emotion instinctively requires that the impact escalate, and assumes closure when peaks and downturns are signaled. All beyond this is anticlimactic, losing attention automatically. The logic of reason is not to be ignored because of this; the two logics can be synthesized in order to provide experiential encounter. . . . This has always been the case with the most powerful preachers of all cultures and schools of theology.[2]

The preacher who gives attention to cognitive logic alone runs the risk of rendering a sermon distant from the senses and experience of the people. On the other hand, attention to emotive logic alone can often end up in the manipulation and abuse of the senses and emotions of the people. Emotive logic ensures that the cognitive truth reaches the experience of people; cognitive logic ensures that the experience of people is engaged with rational coherence and intellectual integrity. Emotive logic insists that the preacher joyfully and ecstatically reinforce the good news of the sermon; cognitive logic mandates that what can be legitimately, joyfully, and ecstatically reinforced is the truth of the good news taught in the main body of the sermon. The partnership of emotive and cognitive logic is critical to the celebrative sermon because only in this holistic partnership is it possible to reach intuitive core belief.

From the perspective of emotional process that reaches core belief, emotive logic and cognitive logic are so intertwined that they are virtually one, and any rigid dichotomy is artificial. If the sermon is an experiential encounter the two logics are two sides of the same coin, though in the various stages of the emotional process of the sermon, one logic tends to come to the forefront, while the other recedes to the background. The receding logic is never totally absent. Rather, receding means the adoption of a monitoring role to ensure that the sermon is the holistic experiential encounter that is necessary to reach core belief. When emotive logic is in the forefront, cognitive logic monitors the emotive content to make sure that there is emotional distance (emotional objectivity), because too little distance in emotional terms breaks down experiential encounter. When cognitive logic is in the forefront, emotive logic monitors the cognitive content to make sure that abstract truth is expressed with sense appeal, because abstraction without sense appeal breaks down experiential encounter. Experiential encounter that intertwines and balances emotive logic and cognitive logic is the path to core belief.

The "Celebration as Ecstatic Reinforcement" chart demonstrates the relationship of cognitive and emotive logic in the various stages of the sermon. First, we must not forget that a key element of emotive logic is identification. Language and images based in sensory data beget identification, and once identification occurs, emotion is stirred and released in the listener. Identification is so critical to emotive logic that it is mentioned alongside emotive logic. Second, we must

8

Celebration as Ecstatic Reinforcement

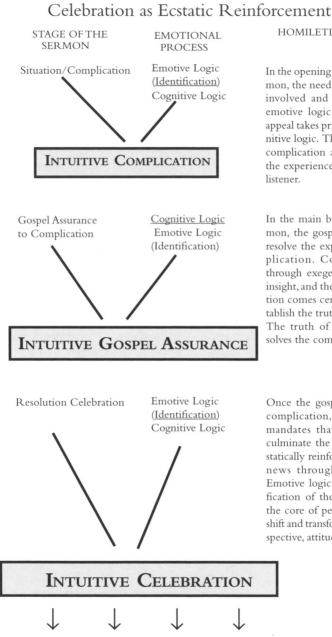

STAGE OF THE SERMON — EMOTIONAL PROCESS — HOMILETIC INTENT

Situation/Complication

Emotive Logic
(Identification)
Cognitive Logic

In the opening stage of the sermon, the need is to get people involved and "on board" so emotive logic through sense appeal takes priority over cognitive logic. The situation and complication are localized in the experience (senses) of the listener.

INTUITIVE COMPLICATION

Gospel Assurance to Complication

Cognitive Logic
Emotive Logic
(Identification)

In the main body of the sermon, the gospel is applied to resolve the experiential complication. Cognitive logic through exegesis, interpretive insight, and theological reflection comes center stage to establish the truth of the gospel. The truth of the gospel resolves the complication.

INTUITIVE GOSPEL ASSURANCE

Resolution Celebration

Emotive Logic
(Identification)
Cognitive Logic

Once the gospel resolves the complication, emotive logic mandates that the preacher culminate the sermon by ecstatically reinforcing the good news through celebration. Emotive logic allows intensification of the good news at the core of people to effect a shift and transformation of perspective, attitude, and feeling.

INTUITIVE CELEBRATION

↓   ↓   ↓   ↓

INFLUENCE ON BEHAVIOR

notice that as cognitive or emotive logic moves to the forefront in the various stages of the sermon, it is the partnership of the receding logic that allows the sermon to reach intuitive core belief in that stage. For example, in the stage of Situation/Complication, emotive logic moves to the forefront, but only in the balance of cognitive logic is the preacher able to locate what we have labeled Intuitive Complication. Last, there is Intuitive Gospel Assurance and then Intuitive Celebration. The type size for each of these intuitive stages gets larger in the chart to show that each intuitive stage builds on the intensity of the previous stage until finally, in Intuitive Celebration, celebration culminates in core belief, releasing the imaginative possibilities of God. Once the imaginative possibilities of God are released in core belief, celebration has a direct influence on behavior.

The preacher who would exclude or limit either emotive or cognitive logic interrupts celebrative emotional process moving to core belief, and severely limits the effectiveness of the sermon. The most effective preachers understand that cognitive logic and emotive logic are not separated in the sermon but are partners that take or yield priority at the appropriate stage of the sermon to facilitate the upward movement to celebration in intuitive core belief. The preacher who would handle celebrative emotional process must thoroughly understand this partnership, be adept at the subtle shifts from one kind of logic to the other throughout the sermon, and be especially comfortable with the culmination in the final stage that moves emotive logic to the forefront for celebration in core belief.

The most effective preachers, composers, teachers, novelists, playwrights, parents, poets, musicians, leaders, etc., of any culture or nation have instinctively recognized and utilized the partnership between emotive and cognitive logic. The African American folk preaching tradition is distinctive in that cognitive and emotive logic are synthesized for the purpose of celebration in the intuitive. The best of African American preaching unifies cognitive and emotive logic and builds toward the culmination of celebration in the final stage of the sermon. The Holy Spirit rides upon this culmination of celebration in the intuitive to shift perspective and transform possibilities. Recognizing the importance of this final stage of celebration for celebrative emotional process, we turn to discuss several guidelines that ensure the balance of emotive and cognitive logic.

THE GUIDELINES OF CELEBRATION

We are making the assumption that we have moved through two stages of the sermon to the place where the gospel has resolved the presented complication of life. We are now ready to move into the final stage of the sermon—celebration. How does the preacher avoid the structural resistance that breaks down the upward movement of celebration in the final stage of the sermon? How does the preacher avoid reintroducing anxiety in the place where anxiety has been resolved, and where the resolution demands to be celebrated? What are some of the guidelines that will help the preacher balance emotive and cognitive logic so that intuitive celebration occurs in core belief? The preacher who would celebrate in the final stage of the sermon must give attention to five basic guidelines: avoidance of new concepts, contagious conviction, affirmative themes, focus on the theme, and timing of impact.

1. *Avoidance of New Concepts.* New cognitive ideas do not belong in celebration, because it is difficult to celebrate and digest new cognitive truth at the same time. Celebration fortifies what has already been taught, explained, and comprehended by emotional reinforcement in the upward flow of the sermon. No *new* cognitive material should be presented in celebration, because people must shut down the emotional flow to grasp new cognitive material. Cognitive material introduced in the final stage of the sermon indicates an emotive downward turn, and hence a return to the main body of the sermon. New cognitive ideas interrupt the upward celebrative emotional flow and therefore must be restricted to the main body of the sermon.

A personal example illustrates how the introduction of cognitive material in the final stage serves to close down celebration. I was guest preacher at a church and had structured the sermon for celebration. The gospel resolved an experiential complication of life, and the people enthusiastically received the resolution. I joyfully reinforced the gospel truth, and the church exploded in praise and thanksgiving to God. There was such an explosion of emotion that I was stunned, lost my equilibrium, and literally did not know what to do. To that point, I had received and accepted the conditioning that taught one to be afraid of emotion, especially free and spontaneous emotion. To handle my own anxiety and reestablish a sense of control, I introduced the following quote by T. S. Eliot:

We shall not cease from exploration
And the end of all our exploring
Will be to arrive where we started
And know the place for the first time.[3]

Though this insightful quote fit with my theme, it had the effect of shutting down the emotive flow because people had to resort to cognitive logic to process the ideas expressed.

My return to the cognitive in the final stage of the sermon signaled a return to the main body of the sermon where cognitive logic was in the forefront. People experienced this return as an abrupt shift, and it had the effect of decisively breaking down the upward movement to celebration. Celebration was crippled beyond repair, and I was never able to restore the emotive flow. The celebrative sermonic design crumbled into ashes, and there was nothing to do but close the sermon, and lean on the tender mercies of God. I am sure that there were people in the congregation who received the gospel from the sermon, but the gospel could have been so much more effective if I had not introduced new cognitive material in the closing stage of celebration.

2. *Contagious Conviction.* Contagious conviction is caught from an infectiously celebrative preacher. By the time the emotional process of the sermon reaches the final stage of celebration, the truth of the sermon should have become conviction for the preacher, and therefore available to be spread contagiously until many are affected.

I can illustrate contagious conviction with another personal example—I recently attended a conference at which a very controversial issue was   discussed. As often occurs when difficult issues are discussed, people engaged in polemics, and the conference split into groups with the attendant emotions of hostility, anxiety, blame, etc. Though very emotional at its core, the discussion was conducted at the level of information. Each group presented their facts, figures, and information to demonstrate that they were confronting the "real issue" and therefore anyone who did not agree with their proposed solution was "not dealing with the real issue."

In the concluding session, a speaker moved the discussion beyond the level of ideas and information to core belief. She did not debate what the real issue was; instead, she presented what she believed and the action she took based on what she believed. She maintained the posture that, whatever one believed, the central question was, did one have the *courage* to confront evil? Her presence articulated that we could debate the real issue forever, but the real question was one of the *spiritual and moral courage* to act on what we said we believed. Without putting it in words, she suggested that we had been tediously arguing about what the real issue was in order to procrastinate the real work. This woman committed her whole life to what she believed, and we were being challenged in core belief to do the same. The polarization was defused because we were encountered and infected by a contagious commitment.

The power of her presentation was more than her obvious rhetorical power. It was more than the fact that she was educated, eloquent, and charismatic. It was more than the information she presented, and she presented penetrating information. Her power was a gut conviction that ordered the information she presented. She was so sure of the gospel that it gave her the courage to act, even if it meant danger and risk to her person. The ultimate power of her presentation was her core belief certainty in the assurance of grace. At the core, she had a contagious conviction, and that conviction infected the group deeply in core belief.

Though she was not a preacher, the emotional process of her presentation reminded me of the role of celebration and of the celebrative preacher in the final stage of the celebrative sermon. Celebration begins with a "celebrant," a person who gets infected (experiences the conviction appropriate to the preaching of the gospel) and then seeks to infect others. The preacher's conviction of the assurance of grace results in joyous celebration (praise and thanksgiving) that spreads from person to person.

The preacher is infected by contagious conviction, but needs a person or persons who are close enough to make intuitive connection and will become quickly infected. Traditionally this phenomenon has been labeled "call and response," but it is the intuitive and participatory connection between preacher and people that pushes the preacher to explore with abandon the creative depths of Spirit-led celebration. Often people will stand up, wave their hands, or punctuate the sermon with positive declarations such as "Amen!," "Go 'head, preacher!," and "Yeah!" in rhythmic cadence with the preacher as an affirmation and celebration of the assurance of grace delivered unto their lives. Without intuitive connection in the hearers, contagious conviction diminishes in the sermon of the preacher. But with intuitive connection, conviction intensifies and becomes more contagious, until others are infected. The more people who are infected, the more contagious the conviction becomes, until contagious conviction spreads from "heart to heart and breast to breast," and many are affected. Celebration in the final stage of the sermon is the rhetorical form to deliver contagious conviction to the core belief of people.

3. *Affirmative Themes.* Celebration must be based in the great affirmative themes of the Bible: mercy, compassion, hope, healing, justice, forgiveness, peace, salvation, and most of all love. There are many magnificent scriptures that serve to exemplify these affirmative themes, but of them all John 3:16–17 comes first to mind:

> For God so loved the world that God gave the only Son, so that everyone who believes in him may not perish but may have eternal life. Indeed, God did not send the Son into the world to condemn the world, but in order that the world might be saved through him.

The heart of the gospel message is the possibility of reconciliation, restoration, and healing, which are affirming of people and the world. If we would celebrate in the final stage of the sermon, we must preach the great healing and empowering themes of the Bible.

It would seem that basing celebration in affirmative themes would be obvious, but though God did not send Jesus the Christ into the world to condemn the world, some Christians condemn others in the name of love. I read an article describing the experience of an African American lesbian author with a Christian attempting to demonstrate God's love. She describes an experience where she took questions from the audience at the conclusion of a lecture:

Eventually I became tired and announced that I'd answer one final question. A young White man wearing a baseball cap waved his hand frantically from the balcony. And there it was: "You and all gays are going to hell. I'm telling you this because God taught me to love you." Then he cited a Bible passage.[4]

The question is not one's theological or moral position on the question of lesbianism, but how one functions with one's position on lesbianism.[5] The young man was well within his right and privilege to believe that lesbianism is a sin, but how he functioned with what he believed is problematic. I believe sentencing people to hell is God's domain and God's prerogative. Condemning people to hell in the name of love is to function negatively and immaturely with one's belief and position. The lesbian author talked about this experience in the context of her understanding of the biblical message of love, even if the Christian considers the behavior sin. She rationalized the difference between what she understood as the biblical standard of love and this young man's demonstration as the ability of some to use religion to suppress what they personally find offensive. She identified the comments as hatred and condemnation masked in the garb of biblical love.

Some preachers function with the same spirit of condemnation in the pulpit. I have heard preachers stir up people by preaching "against" others. Preaching "against" means to vilify or consign to hell persons the group being preached to finds offensive. Preaching against people is the direct and stark opposite of the celebrative gospel message.[6]

There is no question that cheap criticism and clever negativity can be quite effective in bringing an audience to its feet in thunderous applause and hysteria. This can be seen every day on most television talk shows in America, where petty put-downs and scintillating negativity garner audience enthusiasm and the highest ratings. The studio audiences, and I assume the host, network, advertisers, and home viewers as well, are entertained by the malicious name calling, immature personal attacks, and ridiculous fistfights that attempt to pass for growth-producing dialogue and discussion.

The sad truth is that what occurs on some talk shows occurs in some pulpits in the name of the gospel. I have seen preachers engage in negative preaching and people come to their feet in support and applause. I have learned that not all deep feeling and conviction is celebrative; some is vicious and mean-spirited. A negative gospel is never a motivation for true biblical celebration. Preaching against people, or sending someone to hell, is never a motivation for celebration. This may be *emotionalism*, but it is not celebration.

Negative preaching and emotionalism might stir feelings of celebration among the group, but the celebration is false, because it is based upon negative emotions for others. Biblical celebration cannot be based upon negative feelings. Biblical celebration maintains the balance of God's judgment and love, and concludes everything with the experiential encounter of the healing, reconciling, and forgiving love of God.

Some are afraid this means the preacher cannot preach against sin and therefore "lets sinners off the hook," but the gospel affirms personhood and people.[7] The gospel faces people in their sin and invites them to leave it for the life of freedom in Christ. The function of the gospel is to heal and save people. If our preaching functions to condemn and destroy people, regardless of our motivation, it is not the gospel. Therefore, negative preaching and negative criticism do not belong in the celebrative sermon at all, and especially in the final stage of celebration. Helpful criticism belongs early in the sermon, but the further along we are, the more we present biblical affirmation. In the final stage of the sermon, there is only room for a genuine and sincere invitation to the healing, forgiving, and reconciling grace of God.

4. *Focus on the Theme.* The biblical affirmation celebrated must be the exact same affirmation taught and experienced in the main body of the sermon. The temptation is to find material for celebration that is powerfully moving, and use it even if it does not relate to the body of the sermon. This material may allow the people to celebrate, but celebrate what? To be genuine, celebration reinforces the biblical truth already taught in the main body of the sermon. Celebration that does not follow this standard borders on what we earlier labeled emotional manipulation, or emotionalism, which is the raw appeal to emotion, totally abandoning the cognitive logic that is the balancing part of healthy emotion.

There is tremendous pressure in much of the African American church to close the sermon with a powerful crescendo. Because the preacher must "mine" the celebratory good news (chapter 4), and mining is an extremely strenuous and exhausting process, the temptation is to succumb to the pressure and pull a celebration that is at best irrelevant to the sermon, and at worst manipulative of people's experience. In conformity to this pressure, I have seen preachers ride roughshod over the main body of the sermon, totally ignoring the situation, complication, and gospel assurance to spend most of the sermonic discourse moving to a crescendo unrelated to the biblical truth of the sermon. I have seen preachers do an outstanding job developing and teaching the central truth of the text then, yielding to this pressure, achieve celebration no matter what great leaps they had to make to get there.

When we are unwilling or unable to do the hard work of mining true celebration, the temptation is to use tried-and-true celebrative standbys, e.g., a story of conversion or deathbed healing, or "taking people by the cross" (the Calvary-Easter narrative), etc. These standbys can be very appropriately used if they reinforce the truth taught in the main body of the sermon, but otherwise they are simply clichés. It is a great challenge indeed to develop for each and every sermon a celebration which is both powerful and relevant to the truth taught in the body of the sermon. The preacher must take up this challenge weekly, resisting the awesome temptation to resort to raw emotionalism and disguise it as celebration.

5. *Timing of Impact.* Timing of impact is planning and focusing the emotive flow to move the sermon upward to celebration. We all know how important timing is to jokes or stories. Who of us has never felt the sting of embarrassment because we missed the punch line, and the joke or story fell flat on its face? Or who has not felt pleasure when the response to a story or joke indicates that we told it well? Timing of impact suggests that if there is going to be celebration, very careful attention must be paid to "emotive timing." We must weigh every piece of sermonic material to consider its emotive impact.

To properly manage the emotive flow and pace, the hearer's holistic involvement in the sermon must move upward through every stage of the sermon with more and more intensity. Often, whether or not this process occurs has to do with how well we order our sermonic materials. One preacher began a sermon in a way that demonstrates total unawareness of the importance of timing:

> Today, I would like to preach from the parable of the prodigal son, recorded in the fifteenth chapter of Luke. You remember the story! The boy asks for his inheritance, leaves home, and loses everything living riotously. But do not worry, he comes back home in the end.

There is no longer any reason to listen to the sermon, because there is no suspense. The preacher demonstrated poor ordering of sermonic material by resolving the suspense at the start of the sermon. It is the suspense, and the preacher's experiential presentation of the suspense, that helps people to listen. Effective timing is to maintain suspense as long as possible before resolution with the gospel, and the celebration of that resolution. If there is no suspense, there will be very little resolution, and therefore virtually nothing to celebrate. At every point in the sermon, the materials should be structured to maintain suspense that moves upward at resolution to celebration.

While one extreme is to raise suspense and resolve it before the sermon begins, another extreme is to raise suspense and never resolve it. A preacher preached the text of the good Samaritan in Luke 10:

> Our text for today raises the issue of why bad things happen to good people. The man was on his way, minding his own business, and fell among thieves. Why do bad things happen to good people? But, for this morning's sermon, I would like to address the Levites and priests who walked by an injured man on the way to the temple.

The preacher then goes on to address and resolve the issue of going to church and passing wounded people. He never again raises or resolves the issue of why bad things happen to good people. Had I been listening to this preacher, I would have wondered about the issue of bad things happening to good people. I would have felt incomplete because the preacher did not resolve the question that was raised. I strongly believe that the preacher should not raise what the preacher cannot resolve. If the preacher cannot resolve it, does not intend to resolve it given the limits of one sermon, then why bring it up? If the hearers go home with unresolved issues because the preacher never brought resolution, the preacher must shoulder much of the blame for poor preaching. Unresolved issues create unplanned suspense that breaks down the upward flow and diminishes intensity in celebration.

Maintaining suspense as long as possible does not mean, of course, that we save all the good news to the end for "timing of impact." The preacher should not order the sermon with three-fourths solemn material for suspense, and then paste on a celebration. The preacher must be careful to remember that we are talking about being in tune with the heart and core of the gospel. This means that we take the suspense of the bad news seriously, but underneath the bad news is the melody of the gospel. The bad news hurts, the bad news makes us cry, the bad news gives us grief and agony. But the gospel resolves the suspense, and at the point of celebration, this melody moves from the background to take center stage. Though particular notes and measures may be harsh and discordant in the sermonic symphony, only in celebration does the gospel melody develop into full crescendo, and in that crescendo all doubts are settled and all fear is gone.

MATERIALS OF CELEBRATION

What are some of the materials that lend themselves to celebration in the final stage? When designing a celebration, what kinds of raw materials can be used to foster celebration? Celebrative emotive logic comes front and center stage in celebration, which means affirmative and joyous emotion with the beauty and flow of poetry, music, and art are the rule and standard. Poetry, heightened rhetoric, creative imagery, hyperbole, and embellished language are all suitable vehicles for expression of the profoundly joyous and hopeful disposition of celebration.

As an example of materials that lend themselves to celebration, let's review again the celebration of the sermon in "Uncle Wash's Funeral." Upon close inspection, we discover three primary materials of celebration that are woven with imagination and creativity to shape the assurance of grace: (1) the biblical image of Jacob's ladder, (2) the imaginative story of Uncle Wash climbing Jacob's ladder to heaven and meeting the dying thief, and (3) the familiar hymn "There Is a Fountain." When the preacher connects the image of the dying thief in the second verse of the hymn with Uncle Wash's condition as a thief, and allows the dying thief at the top of Jacob's ladder to welcome Uncle Wash in paradise, and all made possible by that "fountain filled with blood . . . where sinners lose all their guilty stain," the assurance of grace explodes within the core belief of the hearers. The imaginative capacity generates celebrative material, and celebrative materials stimulate the imaginative capacity. When celebrative material and imaginative capacity are skillfully handled by the preacher, celebration usually occurs in the core belief of the hearer.

As a general guideline, we can say that any creative and imaginative sensory descriptive material that is capable of expressing joyous and affirmative feeling is substance for celebration. Any material based in sense appeal that puts us in touch with festive and positive emotions is suitable for use in celebration. Any material that triggers the imaginative capacity by releasing affirmation, hope, peace, joy, and love in core belief is potential material for celebration.

With this as a general guideline, there are many, many materials available for celebration: poetry, music, images, metaphors, stories, personal testimony, anecdotes, plays, novels, etc. And then there is the preacher's own spirit, gestures, facial expressions, and personhood that can generate a contagion of celebration. Remember, we said that the preacher was a celebrant, which means the preacher experiences the emotion and conviction appropriate to the preaching experience first, and then invites others to participate as well. The person and celebrative experience of the preacher are material for celebration. Any materials that touch deep and positive emotions within us can be baptized, sanctified, and used as source material for celebration.

Perhaps the best source of materials of celebration is the Bible itself. As we have pointed out throughout this book, the Bible is filled with heightened rhetoric and poetic language that celebrates and exalts God's victory over evil. The imagery and beauty of Habakkuk 3:17–19 is a perfect example of the rich material available for celebration within the Bible:

> Though the fig tree does not blossom, and no fruit is on the vines; though the produce of the olive fails, and the fields yield no food; though the flock is cut off from the fold and there is no herd in the stalls, yet will I rejoice in the Lord. I will exult in the God of my salvation. God, the Lord, is my strength; God makes my feet like the feet of a deer, and makes me tread upon the heights.

This text weaves positive affirmation of trust in God's ability to provide, even in the most difficult of times, around the powerful image of a deer feasting and grazing in high places.

The preacher could preach this text in and of itself because of its rich imagery, or quote the text in the celebration of a sermon on trust and God's ability to provide. In the latter case, the image, metaphor, and heightened rhetoric here could be utilized to reinforce the truth of God's providential care in celebration. Without question the Bible is the best source material for celebration, but the preacher must know it intimately and personally. The more familiar the preacher is with Scripture, and by "familiar" we mean the more that Scripture and scriptural affirmation reside in core belief, the more the preacher can drink from this limitless well of celebrative materials.

Another source of celebrative material is the great music of the church. The great music of the church naturally lends itself to the joyful reinforcement of the truth that has already been taught in the sermon. Much of this great music is already familiar to the people, and many times they have had some emotive history with the music. Therefore, there is less risk that the music will shut down the emotional flow of celebration by going "cognitive." Bringing the known music into the context of the present sermon celebration triggers past positive emotive experiences that aid the present celebration. I have seen preachers time and time again tremendously heighten celebration with the selection of a relevant song that the congregation knows and can easily sing. Second to the Bible itself, music is the best source of celebrative material.

As an example of the great emotive depth of music and its natural ability to celebrate, I would like to illustrate the celebrative power of three different varieties of music: a classical hymn, a traditional spiritual, and a contemporary gospel.

The celebrative power of a classical hymn is best illustrated by a story from the pastoral ministry of André Trocmé, whom we mentioned in chapter 1. Trocmé, his church, and the people of the village of Le Chambon worked to save the lives of Jews from the onslaught of Hitler during the German occupation of France. It was dangerous and risky work, particularly as the Germans began to lose critical battles and started to become nervous of defeat. Vicious crackdowns were ordered on those who aided and abetted the enemy in any way. These crackdowns led to many arrests, placement in concentration camps, and subsequently for some, even death. Two Vichy policemen came to the house of André Trocmé to arrest him for hiding Jews. The word spread quickly in the community that their beloved pastor was being placed under arrest, and people quickly lined the streets. Philip Hallie describes what happened next as the two policeman and Trocmé left Trocmé's home:

> As the three walked west down the street toward the high road that led to the village square, the bystanders began to sing the old Lutheran hymn "A Mighty Fortress Is Our God." A woman named Stekler, sister of a half-Jew who had been arrested and released by the Vichy police, started the singing. The calm, deeply rooted song surrounded the three men, while the villagers closed behind them, and the clop-clop of their wooden shoes, muffled a little by the thin snow, followed them up the street.[8]

The people sang "A Mighty Fortress Is Our God"[9] as they faced the reality that they might not ever see their pastor again.

The moving story of the people's faith and trust in God's ability to overcome evil, even in the midst of being persecuted by evil, could be used in celebration to joyfully and ecstatically reinforce the theme of God's victory over evil in some sermon. But our main focus is the song they sang, and the power of song to celebrate and offer hope in the midst of desperate circumstances. Hallie called the song "calm and deeply rooted." The people had an emotive history in core belief with this song that had to do with centuries of severe persecution for being Protestant in the midst of Catholic France. The person who started the song had a sister who had been arrested and maybe when she sang "A Mighty Fortress Is Our God," she found courage to handle her sister's arrest. She had an emotive history with the song, and offered contagious conviction to Trocmé and the crowd and even to the two Vichy policemen. The emotive history of the woman triggered the emotive history in the people, and despite the night-mare of arrest they had hoped never to see, they were certain that God would win the battle. The church has an extraordinary number of classical hymns that are as moving and available as "A Mighty Fortress Is Our God."

Another very powerful source of celebrative material is the Afri-can American spiritual. Spirituals, made famous by the likes of the Fisk Jubilee Singers, Roland Hayes, Marian Anderson, and Paul Robeson, are known world over for their beauty, simplicity, depth, power, and assurance of grace. The spiritual is the creative, imagina-tive, and celebrative response of the slave to the degradation of sla-very—in Lovell's words, "the free heartbeat of a chained people."[10] Most spirituals are the assurance of grace of the gospel in musical form.

One of the major images in spirituals that carry much power in core belief is the heavenly city, the new Jerusalem that John saw and gave elaborate description of in the Book of Revelation. The city of Jerusalem, the home of Jesus, was a symbol of freedom and a meta-phor for the earthly and heavenly place where a slave could find fulfillment as a free person in a free land. The slave was willing to work and suffer to claim the holy city of Jerusalem. The slave was very sense-descriptive about this city, especially in the spiritual "Oh, What a Beautiful City!"[11]

A careful reading and hearing of the spiritual reveals that the slave believed that in the holy city of Jerusalem, there would be no slavery, racism, death, disease, or other afflictions. There were three gates in the north, three in the south, three in the east, and three in the west— twelve gates to the city representing God's grace to people regardless of race, class, nation, or social status. The slave understood that limits to any city or dominion are established by the gates to the city that protect the borders. This city of Jerusalem was of such stretch and sweep that the gates are the north, south, east, and west. In other words, this city has no borders. Overwhelmed in his or her imagination at the possibility of this city, the slave expansively exclaims, "Oh, what a beautiful city, Oh, what a beautiful city!"

I heard Kathleen Battle and Jessye Norman sing this spiritual, describing the holy city in song, and when they got through, I could say like John, "I saw the new Jerusalem."[12] It was one of the most breathtaking experiences of my life. I caught the contagious conviction of the slave for the holy city of Jerusalem. Through the eloquence of their musical interpretation, they rendered the contagious conviction of the song. I saw the new Jerusalem, and all I could exclaim was, "Oh, what a beautiful city, Twelve gates to the city, hallelu!" Many other African American spirituals carry the contagious conviction of "Oh, What a Beautiful City."

My third example is contemporary gospel music. I once heard a masterful sermon on the rapture that will help demonstrate the stirring power of gospel music. The preacher's text was 1 Thessalonians 4:13–18.[13] At the conclusion of the sermon, and in the midst of powerful celebration and moving crescendo, the preacher quoted from the contemporary gospel song "We Shall Behold Him." The congregation rose in thunderous praise as the preacher skillfully ushered celebrative affirmation to core belief. Just as the preacher finished, a soloist came forward and sang "We Shall Behold Him." With one of the most beautiful voices I have ever heard, she joyfully and ecstatically reinforced the truth taught in the main body of the sermon as she sang:

> The sky shall unfold, preparing His entrance; the stars will applaud Him with thunders of praise; the sweet light in His eyes shall enhance those awaiting; And we shall behold Him, then, face to face. We shall behold him. . . . We shall behold him, face to face in all of his glory. . . . We shall behold him face to face, our Saviour and Lord.[14]

The celebration inside the sermon itself had already built tremendous intensity in my core belief, but when she sang what he preached, tears flowed uncontrollably down my face. They were tears of hope, joy, and thanksgiving, because I could see the assurance of grace. I could literally see the sky unfold and the stars applauding the entrance of my Savior and God. The emotion that flooded my soul was overwhelming, and tears were my release. The more she sang, the more I saw it, and the more I cried, until I gave up trying to maintain any semblance of control. I slumped over in my seat, enfolded by the embrace of the minister next to me, who so graciously understood. Contemporary gospel is a rich source of music that communicates the celebratory affirmation of "We Shall Behold Him."

CELEBRATION AND INTONATION

One more form or vehicle of celebration needs to be discussed before we close this chapter—celebration as intonation. Intonation is the use of musical tone or chant to add another dimension or "wavelength" of celebrative meaning in the final stage of the sermon. For some, musical tone or chant in celebration adds unique shades of joyous and affirmative meaning in core belief. In the African American preaching tradition, intonation is referred to in various ways: "whooping," "tuning," "moaning," etc.[15]

Because intonation has such a major place in the preaching tradition of the African American church, many think it originated and is solely practiced in African American pulpits. Henry H. Mitchell asserts that the early white Baptists of Georgia brought their own preaching tone with them from Massachusetts. Described as a "holy whine," it traces back to the sonorous preaching ministry of George Whitfield during the First Great Awakening (1726–1750s).[16] Whitfield was trained in drama at Oxford and brought tremendous theatrical gifts to the pulpit. Shubal Stearns and Daniel Marshall were converted under the "dramatic" preaching of Whitfield in New England. Later changing over to the immersionist Baptist faith, they launched missions in Winchester, Virginia; Sandy Creek, North Carolina; and Kiokee, Georgia, where Daniel Marshall settled in 1771.

In Kiokee, Daniel Marshall met and converted George Lisle, who in turn founded the first African Baptist congregation at Silver Bluff, Aiken, South Carolina. Lisle also founded the First African Baptist Church of Savannah, Georgia. It is clear that George Lisle and Andrew C. Marshall (later pastor of First African Baptist of Savannah) merged the dramatic and tonal preaching of Daniel Marshall with African traditional religion, narration, and tonal language, and the "whoop" was born in the African American church. Many are surprised to find that though intonation is primarily found in African American congregations, it has historic and present parallels in white Southern culture.

In some major strands in the African American preaching tradition, intonation is considered ridiculous and totally inappropriate for the preaching of the gospel. Other strands value intonation highly, giving the impression that to celebrate at all one has to intone—"if one has not whooped, one has not preached." The fundamental question is not whether "to intone or not to intone" but rather, as with other aspects of the sermon, whether it serves to reinforce the truth already taught in the main body of the sermon. Using intonation without a focus on that truth runs the risk of empty manipulation of feelings. And, as stated earlier, unrelated or irrelevant emotionalism will erase the message and text that the preacher sought to teach, leaving only the celebration vivid in the mind of the listener.

Intonation can be an appropriate and powerful vehicle for celebration when it is natural and authentic to the preacher and congregation, and when it reinforces the truth already taught. But divorced from biblical substance (cognitive logic), it is emotionalism, a cheap replica of celebration. There is no need for unauthentic emotionalism when the gospel is truly preached, because the gospel generates its own genuine emotion and celebration. I have heard powerful sermons with exceptional celebrations in the final stage that involved intonation. I have also heard outstanding sermons with phenomenal celebrations that did not use intonation. Intonation is the Spirit-guided choice of the preacher and the congregation. It is one vehicle, or one form, which some preachers and congregations use in celebration.

Celebration is both *the goal* of the emotional process of the sermon and *the final stage* of the sermon through which the goal is achieved. Celebration is acutely expanded and enhanced by a powerful, moving, and effective celebrative closing in the final stage of the sermon. The preacher who follows the guidelines presented in this chapter in the final stage will balance cognitive and emotive logic, and the emotional process will crescendo to overwrite and/or strengthen the intuitive tapes in core belief. Experiential encounter that balances the cognitive and emotive is the path to intuitive core belief. The goal is to teach as one inspires, and inspire as one teaches.

Three Sermons Illustrating Method

If I talk to anyone at all about preaching, before too long the phrase will slip out of my mouth, "I love preaching!" I absolutely love the challenge of biblical preaching. I love trying to discern the redemptive substance of the gospel, or what healing word the gospel will speak to the situation of human living, especially the condition of suffering and pain. I love trying to figure out the most appropriate rhetorical form or emotional process that will give the gospel the best chance of getting heard. This final chapter gives concrete examples of celebrative sermons that were creative responses to wonderful challenges presented the author by everyday involvement in the life of a congregation and a community of people.

The first sermon, entitled "Extend Your Horizons,"[1] represents the struggle to preach a celebrative sermon in the midst of the tragedy of death and bereavement. Many preachers grapple with delivering the assurance of grace to a family or community racked with the desperate pain of grief and loss. It took several years within my own preaching ministry to develop the knack for mining the assurance of grace for the peculiar experience of death. I offer this funeral sermon as an example of the kind of healing grace that is readily available within the Bible for every experience of human living, even death.

The second sermon, "Where Are the Smiths?," from the text of 1 Samuel 13–14, attempts to discover creative biblical solutions to the massive economic problems encountered by the African American community. Many African American communities are in dire straits because of the lack of a constructive economic base within the community. Rather than simplistically blame our problems on those outside our community, or passively accept the negative and destructive economy of cocaine, crack, and drugs, I attempt to discover positive avenues we can take to secure economic health and viability for our community. I attempt to discover biblically what we can do that will allow God to move on our behalf, and win the battle for economic justice.

The last sermon, "See My Change!," from the text of 2 Kings 5:1–15, is my word of testimony as to how God has brought change into my life through the pain of dipping into the filthy waters and muddy streams of life. In fifteen years of pastoring, there have been and continue to be many painful mistakes and difficult times, but whenever I demonstrate faith through obedience, I find myself healed. Whenever I obey God, whether or not I agree with or understand what God is asking me to do, the conclusion to the process of growth is that I jump out of the muddy stream announcing, "See my change!"

SERMON 1: EXTEND YOUR HORIZONS

The Scriptural Context (John 14:1–3)

(1) Do not let your hearts be troubled. Believe in God, believe also in me. (2) In my Father's house there are many dwelling places. If it were not so, would I have told you that I go to prepare a place for you? (3) And if I go and prepare a place for you, I will come again and will take you to myself, so that where I am you may be also.

The Preaching Worksheet

1. *What does this passage say to me?* Jesus repeatedly announces to the disciples his imminent departure, and the anticipation of the departure stirs feelings of enormous grief, fear, and loss in the disciples. Jesus attempts to calm their fears by proclaiming the good news that (1) God has prepared a glorious place in heaven, and (2) Jesus will come back to take them to this glorious place. Jesus speaks as an eyewitness who has seen and experienced the glorious place firsthand, and encourages the disciples to relieve their grief by trusting him and trusting God.

2. *What does this passage say to the needs of people in our time?* Many people experience tremendous pain and grief at a time of loss, separation, and departure. This text is for our comfort and help in these difficult times. This text reminds us that God has prepared a place for all who believe and trust in the Sovereign. Not only has God prepared the heavenly place, but Jesus is coming back to personally escort us to God's prepared place, where there is no separation, loss, sickness, death, or dying.

3. *What is the "bad news" in the text? What is the "bad news" for our time?* The bad news is that death, loss, and separation are an inevitable part of this life. There is no way for most of us to avoid the pain and agony of loss and bereavement. We all will have times of intense pain and suffering as we experience the inescapable loss of people we love.

4. *What is the "good news" in the text? What is the "good news" for our time?* Though we all experience pain at the time of grief and loss, we can be encouraged by the fact that God has prepared a place. Jesus tells us and assures us that God has provided a heavenly mansion with many rooms. Not only has God provided the mansion, but Jesus will come back and personally escort believers to this glorious place. Trusting God and Jesus is critical to getting through difficult times of loss and bereavement.

5. *Behavioral Purpose Statement*

I propose to experientially illustrate that even though losing someone we love can cause us tremendous pain, Jesus tells us of a glorious place God has prepared that overcomes death, to the end that hearers will find hope, courage, and comfort in times of death and bereavement.

6. *Strategy for Celebration*

a. *What shall we celebrate?* The fact that God has prepared a heavenly place. Christ has seen and experienced the place, and comes back to assure us as an eyewitness.

b. *How shall we celebrate our response in 6a?* The sermon will be ordered for experiential encounter by paralleling Jesus with a teacher I once had who had been around the world and told me many fascinating things about places that I had never seen. I believed the teacher because he had been there and he knew. In times of death, we can find comfort by believing Jesus when he tells us about heavenly mansions, based upon the very simple premise that he been there and he knew.

c. *What materials of celebration shall we use?* The heavenly city of Jerusalem described by John in Revelation 21; various Scriptures about the reality of heaven; various songs that have served to uniquely minister at times of bereavement.

The Sermon Text

I had a teacher once who had been a world traveler. He had spent much of his life visiting distant places and cultures around the world. He took a special interest in me, and made it a point to tell me of his travels. We sat outside talking one evening, and from where we sat I could see a long way across a vacant field. I watched the sun go down, and as it went down, I noticed a line. The line where the sky meets the earth is called the horizon. The horizon looked to me like the end of things, the edge of the world beyond which nothing was. I remembered that many once believed that to go beyond the line was to fall off the edge of the earth. I asked my teacher about things beyond the line.

He told me that the horizon was indeed the place where the sky meets the earth, but a horizon was also the line, limit, or extent of one's experience, outlook, interest, or knowledge. "Travel," he said, "broadens one's horizons." And because he had traveled, he told me of things beyond the line. He told me of huge islands, strange cultures—things of which I had never dreamed. He told me of the mighty Nile and the pyramids in Egypt; he told me of the great ruins of Zimbabwe. He told me of the seven natural wonders of the world. He told me there was a whole lot more beyond that line. He told me to travel one day and extend my horizons by seeing as much as I could. He told me so many unbelievable things. I believed him on the very simple premise that he had been there and he knew.

I believe this casket is a line beyond which we cannot see. Death is a line on the horizons of our souls beyond which we cannot see. Death is the line that limits our physical relationship with someone we love. Death is a line that has taken away our husband, wife, mother, father, uncle, aunt, sister, brother, cousin, neighbor, church member, family member, or friend. Death is a line that has taken our loved one away. I sat there looking across that field, watching the sun go down, and seeing a line. We sit here having watched our loved one go down, and all that is left is a line. We sit and look and ask, is there more? Is this the end? Is death the point beyond which there is no more?

There is a time when we must stand on faith alone. There is a time when we must walk across the line that marks the end of what we can see. There comes a time when we must believe the word of someone who has been there. I know a man and teacher who went across the line that marks the end of what we can see. I know an eternal traveler who went across the line called death, and came back to tell us about what he saw. I know a cosmic voyager who told me so many unbelievable things about reality beyond the line. I believed him on the very simple premise that he had been there and he knew.

Jesus tells us about a place beyond the line. Jesus tells us about heaven, and says there is more beyond the line, and there is so much more. As you sit looking at the line called death, he says to you in John 14:1–3:

> Do not let your hearts be troubled. Believe in God, believe also in me. In my Father's house there are many dwelling places. If it were not so, would I have told you that I go to prepare a place for you? And if I go and prepare a place for you, I will come again and will take you to myself, so that where I am you may be also.

Jesus says, do not let your hearts be troubled and afraid. God has prepared a glorious and wonderful place, a mansion with many dwelling places, or magnificent rooms. The imagery is that of an oriental house where the sons and daughters have grand apartments under the same roof as their parents. God does not leave us as orphans. God has prepared a place where all of God's children can stay with God under the same glorious roof. God has not left us homeless, but prepares a marvelous, glorious, splendid, and spacious mansion for us.

Jesus is not telling you what he has read in a book some-where about heaven. He is speaking with the authority and authentic perspective of an eyewitness. Jesus is not repeating hearsay about heaven, but informing you of what he has seen with his own eyes. He is not speculating about a future life and hope, but he is absolutely certain of what he is speaking because he has already lived there. It is important that you understand that he has already abided there and can speak with exacting detail about what is there. Jesus tells us of the glorious preparation that he and God have made for all of those who believe, and informs us that he is coming back personally to escort believers home. What he says is truly amazing and inconceivable, but I believe him on the very simple premise that he has been there and he knows.

The question of death is matter of faith alone. It is a matter of faith between you and God. Do you believe God? Do you trust Jesus? Do you have faith in Jesus? Many of us have a hard time with faith in God. But I want to remind you that you exercise a tremendous amount of faith to live in this world everyday. Faith is a natural and normal part of our everyday existence. The only question is who or what will you have faith in. For example, let's say that something is wrong with your health. You will probably go to a doctor, and the doctor will diagnose your ailment. The doctor takes out a pad of paper and writes a prescription. Most of the time, we cannot read what is written there, and few of us question the doctor about what is written there. Because we have faith in the doctor, we trust that the prescription will help our healing, and we take that prescription to the phar-macy. There, the pharmacist goes behind a counter that we cannot see, deciphers the handwriting that we cannot read, and mixes ingredients in proportions that we do not under-stand. The pharmacist then types a label informing us to take the prescription three times daily after meals. We go home and do exactly what the pharmacist says without much hesitation. If you will believe and have faith in your pharma-cist and your doctor, why not Jesus? If you can trust your prescription, why not Jesus? Faith is a natural and normal part of our everyday existence. The only question is who or what will you have faith in.

I have faith in Jesus. I believe Jesus today. I trust Jesus today. I know that God has prepared a heavenly place for those who believe where there will be no more dying or mourning or crying or pain. I believe that in that heavenly place God wipes away every tear from every eye. I believe that in that heavenly place the streets are made of gold and the walls of jasper. I believe that the sun or moon is not needed to give light because the glory of God is the light. I believe that every day will be Sunday. I believe there will be no more bad hearts, sickness, or disease, and doctors and hospitals will not be needed because everyone is perfectly whole. I believe Jesus is the resurrection and the life, and nothing that lives in him shall ever die. I believe that now we know in part and see everything in part, but then we shall see face to face. I believe that earth has no sorrow that heaven cannot cure. I believe one glad morning when this life is over, I'll fly away. I believe that we will

Sing the wondrous love of Jesus,
Sing His mercy and His grace;
In the mansions bright and blessed,
He'll prepare for us a place.
When we all get to heaven
what a day of rejoicing that will be.
When we all see Jesus,
we will sing and shout the victory.[2]

SERMON 2: WHERE ARE THE SMITHS?

The Scriptural Context (1 Samuel 13:16–22, 14:13–15, 23)

(16) Saul, his son Jonathan, and the people who were present with them stayed in Geba of Benjamin; but the Philistines encamped at Michmash. (17) And raiders came out of the camp of the Philistines in three companies. . . . (19) Now there was no smith to be found throughout all the land of Israel; for the Philistines said, "The Hebrews must not make swords or spears for themselves"; . . . (22) So on the day of battle neither sword nor spear was to be found in the possession of any of the people with Saul and Jonathan; but Saul and his son Jonathan had them. . . . (1 Samuel 14:6) Jonathan said to the

young man who carried his armor, "Come, let us go over to the garrison of these uncircumcised; . . . for nothing can hinder the Lord from saving by many or by few." . . . (13) The Philistines fell before Jonathan. . . . (15) There was a panic in the camp, in the field, and among all the people; the garrison and even the raiders trembled, the earth quaked. . . . (23) So the Lord gave Israel the victory that day.

The Preaching Worksheet

1. *What does this passage say to me?* The dignity, self-respect, and self-determination of a community is connected to its ability to control and develop smiths (that is, craftspersons generally). The Philistines, who were at war with Israel, severely handicapped Israel's ability to fight by exiling all the blacksmiths (smiths) to Philistia and outlawing any Israelite from practicing as a smith. The lack of smiths severely hurt the Israelite war effort and also the dignity and self-reliance of the Israelite community.

2. *What does this passage say to the needs of people in our time?* Many African American communities, like Israel in our text, have so few smiths that the dignity, self-respect, and self-reliance of the community have seriously eroded, and continue to erode. If the African American community is to be saved, with God's help it must find and develop smiths.

3. *What is the "bad news" in the text? What is the "bad news" for our time?* In face of the lack of smiths and the lack of weapons, the Israelites gave up all hope of victory in battle, and hid from the enemy. The African American community likewise, when faced with few smiths, few weapons, and desperately small odds for victory, sometimes retreats into passivity and self-destructive violence.

4. *What is the "good news" in the text? What is the "good news" for our time?* God used the faith, weapon, and ingenuity of Jonathan to give Israel the victory in the battle, on the way to giving them victory in the war with the Philistines. While Israel was in fear, and complaining about the lack of smiths and few weapons, God used what weapons they did have to win victory. God is never defeated, and always will help God's people when we have faith in God and use what resources we do have in the community.

5.*Behavioral Purpose Statement*

I propose to experientially illustrate, through a case study of Israel's battle with the Philistines, the critical need in the African American community for smiths, to the end that hearers will choose trades as a means through which God will deliver the community from its problems and despair.

6.*Strategy for Celebration*

a.*What shall we celebrate?* We shall celebrate the providence and power of God that is never defeated when God's people battle the enemy with the resources of the community, however meager, coupled with faith in God.

b.*How shall we celebrate our response in 6a?* The sermon will be structured such that the complication of the text, the lack of smiths and weapons in the army, is resolved in the faith, creativity, and ingenuity of Jonathan, who God used to win a battle.

c.*What materials of celebration shall we use?* In response to the faith and ingenuity of Jonathan, God sent an earthquake to win the battle. All God needs is one person.

The Sermon Text

Without embarking on a long litany of statistics, cases, and examples, I trust it is obvious that there is a tremendous amount of frustration and hostility in much of today's African American community. In the majority of the cities of America, the animosity and despondency of African American people are at seemingly all-time-record levels. These powerful emotions cannot and will not be repressed, and therefore they must find expression through either positive or negative channels. Much too often, they are released through negative channels. Either we externalize the hostility and destroy our neighborhoods with violent crime, senseless murder, alcohol abuse, drug traffic, gang warfare, and the physical, sexual, and emotional abuse of women and children, or we internalize the frustration and destroy our neighborhoods with passivity and hopelessness, adopting the attitude that we are powerless to change anything. Because we perceive ourselves to be powerless, we look for someone outside the community to save the community—the federal government, another Martin Luther King Jr., or a Malcolm X, the school system, social service agencies, the President, etc. We look for anyone but ourselves.

Rather than spend an inordinate amount of time detailing the negative expressions of frustration and hostility, I would rather try to ascertain biblical solutions to these problems. What are the positive and creative responses African Americans can choose to the frustration and hostility in the African American community? How can African Americans use these emotions positively to build and reconstruct, rather than destroy and tear down? How can African American people reclaim their dignity, their self-respect, and their right of self-determination, and become full and equal participating members in American society? I want to address these questions by looking at a biblical case study, in which the Israelite community faced some of the same struggles that face much of the African American community today. There are many parallels between the plight of the African American community and the Israelite community in its battle with the Philistines in 1 Samuel 14–17.

In the backdrop of our text from 1 Samuel, Saul had just become the king of Israel, but Israel was under domination by the Philistines. The Philistines were free to march anywhere in Israelite territory because previous victorious confrontations had allowed them to establish several strategically placed military outposts. The Philistines marched to Michmash, the very heart of Israelite territory, and several miles from Saul's hometown and its capital, Gibeah. Preparing to battle the Philistines and overthrow the domination, Saul chose three thousand men. Two thousand men went to Michmash with Saul, and one thousand with Saul's son Jonathan to Gibeah. Jonathan engaged the Philistine troops at Gibeah and was victorious.

In response to the victory of Jonathan, the Philistines mustered three thousand chariots, six thousand horsemen, and what looked to the Israelites like "troops as numerous as the sand on the seashore." In addition to their advantage in numbers and equipment, the Philistines had superior weapons. The Philistines had the wisdom to gain a monopoly in the trade of blacksmiths throughout the whole region. The Philistines had closed down all the blacksmith shops in Israel.

They transplanted the Israelite smiths to Philistia, and forbade anyone in Israel to take up the trades of working in brass or iron. This prevented the Israelites from making weapons of war to fight against the Philistines. It also handicapped them economically because the Israelites were now dependent upon Philistine smiths for common services such as sharpening knives and plows. When they went to Philistia for the services of a smith, they paid exorbitant prices. Besides the huge economic toll on the community, the result of the monopoly of smiths was that, at the time of battle, there were only two people in the entire Israelite army who had weapons, Saul and Jonathan. How could they possibly hope to win facing a bigger and better equipped army? How could they secure a victory, when only two soldiers had arms?

Sizing up the entire situation, the people of Israel were terrified. The text says that when they saw how difficult their situation was, they hid in caves, behind rocks, in holes in the ground, in tombs and cisterns, and some went into the land of Gad and Gilead for safety. The people despaired, expecting a total and crushing defeat because only Saul and Jonathan had weapons. Saul was as terrified and powerless as the people. Many soldiers were also terrified and deserted the army. The number of Saul's troops dwindled to six hundred.

The situation of Israel closely parallels the situation in many African American communities today. The African American community suffers deeply in its battle for self-respect and self-determination because there are so few smiths—that is, workers skilled in a trade. The battle is perilous and bleak because there are so few craftspeople in African American communities, and the people are caught in despair and hopelessness. Parallel to the Philistines exiling and outlawing smiths is the painful history of discrimination, whereby it was against the law for African Americans to enter trades and unions. And what the law could not achieve to keep African Americans out, many resorted to violence and intimidation to accomplish. The result has been almost a total monopoly of the trades by white workers. African Americans have been banned from the trades and handicapped in their efforts to make their own communities economically viable.

Realizing the tremendous odds against victory, realizing that crushing defeat is imminent, many in the African American community hide in the suburbs, corporate jobs, academic enclaves, and the consumer culture of conspicuous consumption; the soldiers of the community flee to other communities for safety. With the odds of victory so small, many of those who remain in the community negatively channel their fear, hostility, and frustration in violence and a defeated powerlessness. How can the African American community win against such devastating emotional foes as hopelessness and powerlessness? How can an army win a battle when the inner spirit of the army is already defeated? Let's go back to Israel and notice the outcome of the Israelite battle, and discern whether we can learn some positive lessons that will aid the African American community.

What we see in First Samuel is how God used Jonathan to win an Israelite victory. The text says while all the Israelite army, people, and Saul were in disarray, Jonathan exhibited great courage and faith in God. Based on the bold conviction that "nothing can hinder the Lord from saving, whether by many or by few," Jonathan secretly took his armor bearer to the Philistine outpost. Jonathan was convinced that God could win with two soldiers or three thousand soldiers, that numbers did not mean very much to God. Jonathan was not intimidated. Based on his faith, he constructed a plan through which God could win the battle.

It seems that Jonathan found a very narrow point through a ravine where only one Philistine soldier could pass at a time. After inducing the Philistine troops into battle, he and his armor bearer were able to pick off Philistines one by one as they came through the ravine, and kill twenty men. The Philistines were surprised and retreated from Jonathan. As they retreated, there was an earthquake, which confirmed to the Philistines that God was on the side of Israel and heightened their panic. This heightened terror resulted in several other Philistine garrisons falling apart, and the Philistine camp was defeated and in total confusion. The text stressed that Jonathan had nothing to do with the earthquake. It was sent by God. Jonathan was the instrument God used, but the writer is clear that it was God's battle and God's victory. In response to Jonathan's ingenuity and faith, God arose, and God's enemies were scattered.

Saul's lookout men saw the Philistine army melting in all directions. Saul called for the Ark of God, assembled the troops, and proceeded with the mop-up work. As Saul was assembling the troops for battle, the panic and terror in the Philistine camp got worse and worse, with even more Philistine troops in retreat. Israel rose and defeated the retreating Philistines. The people who had hidden in caves, holes, etc., came out and joined the battle. The folk who had deserted and hidden behind Philistine lines joined in the victorious surge. So God rescued Israel.

This text suggests to the African American community that we need some Jonathans and armor bearers who have courage and faith in God to win the battle. What we need are people who will not fear and panic, but people who will use their means, however small, and believe that God will win the victory. What we need are people who will have the bold conviction that "nothing can hinder the Lord from saving, whether by many or by few." We need more people like Jonathan, the catalytic agent who started the victory with the faith to fight twenty men strategically at a ravine. What the African American community needs is the same kind of strategy to pick off negative expressions of fear and hostility at the ravine of community life. The African American community needs to believe God can use the resources in the hands of the community to win the battle. The African American community needs more smiths.

The modern trend in the African American community is to make a big deal out of education and degrees. I made a big deal about them because I once thought education was the way to help our community prosper and grow strong. And it is one of the ways to make our community prosper. But now I more fully realize that behind many of these degrees are an army of maids mopping floors and short-order cooks flipping pancakes. I did not realize how many people sacrificed to send sons and daughters, nieces and nephews to college. I have come to deeply believe that smiths are as important to the community as the educated and the professional.

We have assumed that those in the trades are the economic and social second class. We do not realize that some craftspeople make more than some school principals. My refrigerator broke down the other day, and the man who came out to fix it charged me fifty dollars just to pull up to the front door. He had not even looked at the refrigerator, and already I owed him fifty dollars. After that he charged me by the hour for the labor, and that did not include parts. When I got the bill, I knew this man was not part of the economic second class. If you think I am wrong, call a plumber, an electrician, a bricklayer, an automobile mechanic, etc., and see how much you will pay. You will discover that smiths are not economically second class. There are many craftspeople who make a nice living for themselves and their families.

The African American community is trying to tell all the kids they need to go to college and get an education. But college is not for everybody, and the community needs some smiths. There are many fine, upstanding people who will not go to college, but if they could take up a trade, they would do just as well as the college graduate and add just as much to the community. The community needs smiths, people like Jonathan and the armor bearer who used what little weapons they had (what the trades had generated) to be available for God to use and get the victory. We need Jonathans who will take up a trade and use that trade to strike a blow for strength and health in the African American community. We need Jonathans who will strategically battle, and trust that God will cause an earthquake. We need more Jonathans in the trades who use ingenuity and faith to win for the community. We need some electricians, dental assistants, x-ray technicians, computer specialists, carpenters, roofers, tilers, asphalt and paving people, draftspeople, food service managers, construction estimators, data processors, cartographers, etc. We need to channel our negative passive and aggressive frustration by developing smiths in our communities. The crime, the hate, the passivity, and the self-destruction would go down in our communities if we had more smiths.

This text clearly demonstrates that God will take the smallness of our efforts and win a victory beyond our imagination. We do not have to wait on anybody to come and rescue us. Everybody and everything we need is right here, us and God. We do not have to kill and maim each other because of the unreleased frustration and hostility. We do not have to be involved in the drug culture to make ourselves economically viable. We do not have to chemically abuse ourselves and our families to gain dignity and respect. We can get a trade, and raise the quality of life in our community. We can make a difference. If we join hands with God, we can make a difference. There is nothing that can hinder God from saving, whether there are thousands or there are two. If we will participate in the battle with hope and imagination, God will arise.

God will get involved. God has the welfare of the people already arranged. God has our freedom already established. We are not by ourselves. God is with us. God watches over us. God will win for a community that needs peace, healing, freedom, and self-determination. God will win the battle, if we have faith and ingenuity to begin. God will arise. For God to arise, we need a catalytic agent and instrument. What God needs is modern Jonathans who will strategically confront the enemy with cleverness, conviction, cunning, and confidence. God will send earthquakes. God does not need the odds to be in our human favor to win. God can win, even when the vast majority of the community is caught up in fear and despair. Numbers do not make a big difference for God. Nothing can hinder God from saving, whether by many or by few. All God needs is one. God will arise if there is one. I trust that the Jonathan God needs to arise is you.

SERMON 3: SEE MY CHANGE!

The Scriptural Context (2 Kings 5:1–15)

(1) Naaman, commander of the army of the king of Aram, was a great man and in high favor with his master, because by him the Lord had given victory to Aram. The man, though a mighty warrior, suffered from leprosy. (2) Now the Arameans on one of their raids had taken a young girl captive from the land of Israel, and she served Naaman's wife. (3) She said to her mistress, "If only my lord were with the prophet who is in Samaria! He would cure him of leprosy." . . . (9) So Naaman came with his horses and chariots and halted at

the entrance of Elisha's house. (10) Elisha sent a messenger to him saying, "Go wash in the Jordan seven times, and your flesh shall be restored, and you will be clean." (11) But Naaman became angry and went away, saying, "I thought that for me he would surely come out, and stand and call on the name of the Lord his God, and would wave his hand over the spot and cure the leprosy. (12) Are not Abana and Pharpar, the rivers of Damascus, better than all the waters of Israel? Could I not wash in them, and be cleansed?" He turned and went away in a rage. (13) But his servant approached him and said to him, "Father, if the prophet had commanded you to do something difficult, would you not have done it? How much more, when all he said to you was, 'Wash, and be clean?'" (14) So he went down and immersed himself seven times in the Jordan, according to the word of the man of God; his flesh was restored like the flesh of a young boy, and he was clean. (15) Then he returned to the man of God, he and all his company; he came and stood before him and said, "Now I know that there is no God in all the earth except in Israel."

The Preaching Worksheet

1. *What does this passage say to me?* Naaman was a leper and desperately wanted to be healed, because as a leper he was untouchable. Naaman discovered through the prophet Elisha that God had the power to heal, if he had the faith to do exactly what God said. The question was one of Naaman's willingness to exercise faith and obey the prophet's command, even if Naaman did not agree with or understand the command. Naaman's pride and arrogance collided with his need for the healing that can only be secured by faith demonstrated in obedience.

2. *What does this passage say to the needs of people in our time?* Many of us are lepers, find ourselves untouchable, and desperately want to be healed. The question is not God's power, but whether we have the faith to follow God's commands, even if we do not agree or understand. Our faith collides with our pride and arrogance, and we must decide if we will do exactly what God said. If we have the faith, then we will be healed and changed.

3. *What is the "bad news" in the text? What is the "bad news" for our time?* Naaman's pride and arrogance almost resulted in missing the

blessing of healing. Because of Naaman's pampered perspective, he almost refused to go down and dip seven times. Many of us, like Naaman, have pride and arrogance, and when God tells us to do something, we decide that we know what is best for our healing. Our pride and arrogance place us on the border of missing the blessing of healing because we will only do what we agree with or understand.

4. *What is the "good news" in the text? What is the "good news" for our time?* The power of God is available to heal and change us if we follow God's command. When we exercise our faith, regardless of how ridiculous we think the instructions are, or regardless of whether we agree, God will heal and change us. If we exercise our faith by obedience, then we will be able to say to the world, "See my change!"

5. *Behavioral Purpose Statement*

I propose to experientially illustrate the healing journey of Naaman, from pride and arrogance to willingness to obey the prophet's command, to the end that hearers will move from the pride and arrogance of their own perspective to obedience and faith in God.

6. *Strategy for Celebration*

a. *What shall we celebrate?* The power of God that is available to heal us of our sin and leprosy. The power of God is actualized by discarding our pride and arrogance and exercising our faith by explicitly obeying God's commands. We will then be healed and testify to God's power by proclaiming, "See my change!"

b. *How shall we celebrate our response in 6a?* We shall order the sermon for experiential encounter through the intuitive form of situation-complication-resolution-celebration. Situation: Naaman was a leper and wanted to be healed. Complication: The prophet Elisha prescribed healing, but Namaan's pride and arrogance almost forced him to walk away. Resolution: Despite misgivings and doubt, Naaman dipped seven times and was healed. Celebration: Naaman testified that there is no other God than the God of Israel.

c. *What materials of celebration shall we use?* Naaman's testimony to the God of Israel and testimony to the world about the power of the God of Israel contained in the phrase "See my change!"

The Sermon Text

Naaman was a Syrian, and the commander-in-chief of the army of the king of Aram. He was a man of great valor, highly respected by the king and all the people, because the army had one victory after another under his powerful leadership. Naaman was so successful at war that the Hebrew writer of 2 Kings drew the astonishing conclusion that this pagan, this uncircumcised gentile, this unbeliever, had God on his side. God had to be at work, because nobody could win this many battles without God going before them.

God allowed Naaman to win another battle, and as part of the spoils of victory, he took an Israelite servant girl into his home to serve his wife. She noticed the suffering of Naaman, noticed his isolation and pain. She looked past his wealth, fame, power, and military skill and saw the hurt of his loneliness. Thank God for the humble and unpretentious people in our lives who sincerely love and care about us, and see our inner need! She went to Naaman's wife and told her she knew somebody, who knew somebody, who could take care of her husband's condition. There was a prophet in Israel who knew something about healing. If Naaman went to the prophet, he could be healed of his leprosy.

Leprosy in biblical times was an infectious disease much akin to AIDS today. It was a fungal condition that caused patches of discoloration and thickening of the skin, accompanied by ringworms and psoriasis that made the skin itch and peel, often forming sores. Leprosy was greatly feared, and therefore people violently avoided lepers. The clothing, housing, and possessions of people infected with the fungus were called unclean. Lepers were mandated to wear torn clothing, to keep their hair disheveled, and cover the lower part of their faces and cry out, "Unclean! Unclean!" in order to avoid contact with others. There was tremendous fear of infection, and since there was no cure, there was only isolation of the infected. Wherever possible, lepers were herded into colonies on the outskirts of town or completely outside town boundaries. The leper was an outcast, a reject, and a misfit. They were the wretched of the earth.

Naaman would have been treated just like every other

leper, except that he was a mighty soldier. Because of his military skill, he had the fame, power, and wealth to avoid being treated like a typical leper. He had more privileges than any of the worldwide leper population. But despite everything he had, he experienced himself as having nothing, because as a leper he was untouchable.

Untouchable! People respected him, felt genuine sympathy for his tragic condition, and treated him well, but no one touched him. People smiled at him, were cordial, greeted him politely and respectfully, but nobody touched him. Nobody shook his hand. Nobody caressed his face. Nobody got close enough to allow themselves to be accidentally touched by him. Naaman hugged no one and no one hugged Naaman. People kept their distance, and it hurt Naaman deeply. Naaman had not been touched with deep caring and affection by another human being in a very long time. He had everything, wealth, fame, and power, and yet he experienced himself as having nothing, because he lacked a touch that could reach his soul.

So Naaman went to the king, told him what the servant girl had said, and asked for a leave of absence. The king gave him permission to go. Naaman packed ten talents of silver, six thousand shekels of gold, and ten sets of festal garments, and left for Israel. The king of Aram wrote a letter to the king of Israel stating that he was sending his servant to him that he might be cured of leprosy. The king of Israel got the letter and panicked. He thought it was a trick to set up war, because he did not have the power to heal anybody, and he did not know anybody, who knew anybody, who could heal anybody. He tore his clothes and fell before God.

The prophet Elisha heard that the king had torn his robes, and sent word to the king saying, "Let him come to me, that he may learn that there is a prophet in Israel." God always has a witness, so the prophet tells the king not to worry. When Naaman arrived, the king sent him to Elisha's house in Samaria.

Naaman followed the king's instructions and went down to the house of the prophet. Naaman and his entourage stopped at Elisha's front door with their horses and chariots, with ten talents of silver, six thousand shekels of gold, and ten sets of festal garments. Naaman got out of his elegant chariot, and stood outside as his servant went in to announce his arrival. Because of his status and position, Naaman expected the red carpet to be rolled out. Naaman expected a personal audience with appetizers, fine dining, and stately protocol. Elisha did none of that. Elisha did not even bother to come out. He sent a messenger back out to announce to Naaman to go down to the Jordan and wash seven times, and he would be healed. Naaman got highly upset, and lost his composure.

Naaman got upset because this was a major and disrespectful breach of basic commander-in-chief protocol. Naaman said, "I thought that for me he would surely come out" (v. 11). Naaman was one of the most powerful men in the world, and Elisha had the audacity to send a servant out with such an important message! A man of Naaman's status and position, who has come all this way, with all this entourage, with all of this silver and gold, these festal garments, the very least the prophet could do was come out and greet him personally. It was the height of disrespect and insult to send a servant out and receive Namaan without the royal treatment to which he was accustomed. Naaman was enraged.

If we look at the source of Naaman's rage, Naaman is part of what could be called the "pastor-only crowd." Those in the pastor-only crowd believe that only the pastor can heal, and they cannot be healed unless they have a personal audience with the pastor. The pastor-only crowd take stock of their status and position, and while it is true that pastor Elisha cannot receive everyone, they think their status and position gives them the right to be received. Never mind that deacons and other ministers come to hospital to pray for the member and the family. If the pastor does not come out to pray, then the pastor-only crowd has not been prayed for. If pastor Elisha does not come out to preach, then the pastor-only crowd has not been preached to. Naaman almost missed his blessing looking for a personal visit by pastor Elisha. Naaman did not realize that God has many servants, and God can send a blessing by a deacon, an usher, a trustee, or whoever. Do not miss your blessing waiting for the pastor!

Do not miss your blessing because God does not always send the blessing the way you want, by whom you want, and when you want! God has many servants, and many vehicles and channels of delivering a blessing. Do not miss God's blessing because of your pride.

Second, Naaman did not expect that he would have to do anything to be healed. He said, "I thought that he would surely come out to me and stand and call on the name of the Lord his God, wave his hand over the spot, and cure me of my leprosy." Naaman wanted to be healed, but he did not think he had to do very much to get a healing. He thought if pastor Elisha jumped, danced, shouted, and waved his hands, and called on the name of his God, then Naaman would be healed. Naaman thought that if pastor Elisha's choir sang gloriously, and pastor Elisha's deacons prayed until the power of God came down, that he would be healed. He did not believe that he had to participate in the healing. He did not understand that he had to exercise his faith to get a healing. He believed that the pastor's faith would get him healed. Naaman did not understand that we must risk a tremendous amount of ourselves to get healed. Healings are not cheap, free, or based upon someone else's effort. It costs an enormous amount of faith and risk from the person if God is going to effect a healing.

Third, he thought that he knew best where to get his healing. He asked, "Aren't there rivers in Damascus that are better than the waters of Israel?" The Jordan was dirty, muddy, and unclean, and back in his homeland the water was clear as crystal. How could muddy and filthy water bring forth a healing? Surely the crystal-clear springwater back in Damascus was necessary for healing leprosy! If I had been the prophet, I would have asked him, "If the waters were so healing at home, why did you come here? Why didn't you get in those waters when you were there?" I would have told Naaman, "Don't write prescriptions if you do not know anything about healing." I would have helped Naaman to understand that the waters were only incidental to the healing. The waters did not have any healing properties for leprosy, neither the Jordan nor the rivers in Damascus. The power was in exercising faith, and obeying God's command whether or not one understood it, or agreed with it. The power of God would become operative in Naaman's life by his doing exactly what God said, even if it seemed foolish.

At the core of Naaman's rage, Elisha triggered something deeply buried in Naaman. He interpreted Elisha's treatment of him as rejection, and it brought back all the other times that he had been rejected. The fact that pastor Elisha would not come out triggered all the times people would keep their distance and not touch him. It triggered all the pain and hurt he had suffered all these years. It triggered all the loneliness and agony at being untouchable. Years of hurt and bitterness turned into uncontrollable rage and Naaman stormed off.

As Naaman was headed back to Aram, one of his servants caught up with him and said, "If he had told you to do some great thing you would have done it. Why do you scoff at the small thing?" Thank God for the humble, unpretentious people in our lives that speak the truth to our hurt, arrogance, and folly! Thank God for the humble and unpretentious people in our lives who sincerely love and care about us, and see our inner need! The servant tells Naaman, "The important thing is not the River Jordan, but the last part of the sentence, 'wash and be cleansed.'" It was the beauty, simplicity, and truth of what the servant said that forced Naaman to heed the servant's words.

So Naaman went down and dipped himself in the River Jordan. The water was more muddy and filthy than he had heard, and he detested what he saw. He was repelled by the stench and polluted condition of the river, and he almost vomited at the thought that he would have to go down in that. He was accustomed to the very best of clear water. He bathed in clear springwater at exactly the right temperature. After the bath, he wrapped himself in the finest of hot towels and rubbed himself down with expensive, soothing lotions. He had come from all that to this. Though he was repelled to the pit of his stomach, he remembered what the prophet and his servant had said, and forced himself to go down.

After the first three times, he looked at his hands, and

there was no change. He began to feel foolish. He would just go back to where he came from. He felt embarrassed, humiliated, and stupid. He rationalized that being a leper was not so bad—after all he had his fame and wealth. But he looked at his servant standing there on the riverbank, praying that his master would be healed. Thank God for the humble and unpretentious people in our lives who sincerely love and care about us, and see our inner need!

He went down for the fourth time, and the mud and dirt had now gotten down in all the sores. It stung, and he could feel the infection and the disease. His whole body cried for relief. How do mud and filth help heal? How do stench and refuse cure leprosy? He would die from the infection before he would get healed. He decided to go home, and he raised himself up to leave. Then he heard his servant say: "Naaman, hold on! There is no power in the water, none in the muddy stream. The power comes from doing exactly what God says." And Naaman remembered what the prophet said: "Dip seven times." His servant reminded him, "When God says seven, do exactly what God says."

He went down the fifth time, and his body was still covered with sores. He went down the sixth time. The songwriter said:

Six times in the Jordan, six times so strange;
six times he looked at himself, six times no change.[4]

He wondered if he could be free if he did not dip the seventh time. He doubted that God's promise would come true, even if he did dip the seventh time. The moment of truth was at hand, would he dip the seventh time? He looked over at his servant and the servant said: "When God says seven, six will not do." He went down the seventh time, all the way down in the water this time. He began to feel something new. There was a tingling all over him, and it was not the tingling of infection and disease. It was the feeling of healing. He could feel sores being healed, ringworms melting and leaving his body, and the itch removed. He felt the psoriasis leave, and realized that he had been changed. And this was what he had wanted all his life. This is what he had longed for, hoped for, and prayed for—to be changed. He realized that he had been healed. He could touch people, and people could touch him. He could hug people and people could hug him. He could caress someone's face and someone could caress his. When he realized the beauty of the new future available to him, he jumped up out of the bottom of that muddy river shouting at the top of his voice: "Changed! Glory, hallelujah! Changed! Skin like a newborn baby! Changed! A wonderful change has come over me! I have been changed! See my change!"

He looked at his servant praying on the bank of the stream, and cried to him, "See my change!" He was so astonished and so amazed and so grateful that all he could say was "See my change!" God had done something miraculous for Naaman, and he could not keep it to himself. He had to tell everyone, "See my change! Look at what happened to me! Glory Hallelujah! Changed!" Naaman went back to pastor Elisha's house, and all along the way, he would say to everyone he met, "See my change!" He said to pastor Elisha, "Skin like a newborn baby! See my change! I know that there is no other God than the God of Israel."

See my change!

Notes

1. Celebrative Design and Emotional Process

1. Andrew W. Blackwood, *The Fine Art of Preaching* (New York: Macmillan, 1937); John A. Broadus, *On the Preparation and Delivery of Sermons*, 4th ed. rev. by Vernon L. Stanfield (San Francisco: Harper & Row, 1979).

2. Quoted in Henry H. Mitchell, *Black Preaching: The Recovery of a Powerful Art* (Nashville: Abingdon Press, 1990), 34 (emphasis added).

3. True celebration is the African American preaching tradition at its zenith and best. It is not the intention of this work to gloss over, excuse, or pretend that there are not excesses of celebration that result in emotional manipulation and downright abuse of the gospel. It is rather our purpose to focus on the strength, beauty, and richness of the *best* of celebrative design.

4. Henry H. Mitchell, *Celebration and Experience in Preaching* (Nashville: Abingdon Press, 1990).

5. Edwin H. Friedman, "Theater and Therapy," *The Family Therapy Networker* 8, no. 1 (January–February 1984): 2 (emphasis added).

6. For a detailed discussion of emotional field, or emotional process, see Edwin H. Friedman, "Bowen Theory and Therapy," in *Handbook of Family Therapy*, vol. 2, ed. Alan S. Gurman and David P. Kniskern (New York: Brunner/Mazel, 1991), 134–70.

7. Friedman, "Theater and Therapy," 2.

8. Philip Hallie, *Lest Innocent Blood Be Shed* (New York: Harper & Row, 1979), 171.

9. Amos N. Wilder, *Early Christian Rhetoric: The Language of the Gospel* (New York: Harper & Row, 1964).

10. Wellford F. Hobbie, "The Play Is the Thing: New Forms for the Sermon," *Journal for Preachers* 5, no. 4 (1982): 18.

11. For more discussion of the role of reason in begetting faith, see Mitchell, *Celebration and Experience in Preaching*, 21–32.

12. Ibid., 39.

13. H. Grady Davis, *Design for Preaching* (Philadelphia: Fortress Press, 1985), 22.

14. David Buttrick coined the phrase "moves-in-consciousness," or "moves" in his classic work *Homiletic: Moves and Structures* (Philadelphia: Fortress Press, 1987).

15. For discussion of various forms, see Mitchell, *Celebration and Experience*, 77ff.

16. Hobbie, "The Play Is the Thing," 17.

17. Davis, *Design for Preaching*, 4.

18. V. E. Frankl, "Paradoxical Intention: A Therapeutic Technique," chap. 12 in *Psychotherapy and Existentialism: Selected Papers on Logotherapy* (New York: Simon & Schuster), 1967.

19. Richard H. Armstrong, "Reversals: Their Care and Feeding," *Georgetown Family Symposia* 1 (1971–1972): 139.

20. Ibid.

21. Glenn N. Scarboro, "The Delusions of Differentiation: Notations on Family Process," in *The Therapist's Own Family*, ed. Peter Titelman (Northvale, N.J.: Jason Aronson, 1992), 81.

22. Murray Bowen, *Family Therapy in Clinical Practice* (Northvale, N.J.: Jason Aronson, 1990).

23. Friedman, "Bowen Theory and Therapy," 153.

24. Quoted in Mitchell, *Black Preaching*, 34.

2. A Theology of Celebrative Preaching

1. Primarily, chapters 1–4 of the Gospel of Luke and chapters 1–4 of the Gospel of Matthew record the preparation of Jesus.

2. See Otto Kaiser, *The Book of the Prophet Isaiah*, 2d ed., 3 vols., *Isaiah 1–12, Isaiah 13–39, Isaiah 40–66*, trans. John Bowden (Philadelphia: Westminster Press, 1983).

3. We must take note that celebration is evidenced in both the Hebrew Scriptures and the New Testament. The celebration of Moses and Miriam upon deliverance of the Hebrews from Egyptian captivity in Exodus 15; David's unapologetic dance at the return of the Ark of the Covenant in 2 Samuel 6:14; and this text from Isaiah 61 are examples of a rich tradition of celebration in the Hebrew Scriptures.

4. For the narratives involving Mary Magdalene see Luke 8:2; Mark 15:40–47; John 19:25; Matthew 27:61, 28:1; Mark 16:9; and John 20:11–18.

5. For a magnificent discussion of joyous emotions of the New Testament church see John Koenig, *Charismata: God's Gifts for God's People* (Philadelphia: Westminster Press: 1978), 48–70.

6. It may be that most modern churches bear little resemblance to the celebrative community, but we must acknowledge that true Christian community is noticeably celebrative.

7. Koenig, *Charismata*, 54ff.

8. James Dunn, "Models of Christian Community in the New Testament," *The Church Is Charismatic*, ed. Arnold Bittlinger (Geneva: World Council of Churches, 1981), 103–8.

9. Ibid., 105.

10. Ralph Martin, *The Spirit and the Congregation: Studies in 1 Corinthians 12–15* (Grand Rapids: Eerdmans Publishing Co., 1984), 65.

11. Ibid., 66.

3. THE DYNAMICS OF CELEBRATION

1. Wyatt T. Walker, *Somebody's Calling My Name* (Valley Forge: Judson Press, 1979), 22.

2. O. Richard Bowyer, Betty L. Hart, and Charlotte A. Meade, *Prayer in the Black Tradition* (Nashville: Upper Room Press, 1987), 49–50.

3. "Go Down, Moses," traditional Negro spiritual, located in Thomas P. Fenner, *Religious Folk Songs of the Negro* (Hampton, Va.: The Institute Press, 1909), 199.

4. Martin Luther King Jr., "I've Been to the Mountaintop," April 3, 1968, speech in Memphis, in James W. Washington, *A Testament of Hope: The Essential Writings of Martin Luther King Jr.* (San Francisco: Harper & Row, 1986), 286.

5. It did not escape notice that when the Berlin Wall fell, and when students marched in Tiananmen Square in China, they sang the battle hymn of the civil rights movement "We Shall Overcome."

6. Cathy DeForest, "The Art of Conscious Celebration: A New Concept for Today's Leaders," in *Transforming Leadership: From Vision to Results*, ed. John D. Adams (Alexandria: Miles River Press, 1986), 215–32.

7. Steven Spielberg film, *The Color Purple* (Burbank: Warner Home Video, 1987).

8. Alice Walker, *The Color Purple* (New York: Washington Square Press, 1982).

9. Although too much emotion, thinking, or physical distance can inhibit experiential encounter, too much closeness can also limit the objectivity and awareness necessary for experiential communication. There is the tension and danger of being "underdistanced" or "overdistanced." The underdistanced person jumps up on the stage and saves the heroine from the villain; it is the sports fan who throws oranges at the referee or the parent who interferes in their son's or daughter's wedding by taking over all the arrangements. The overdistanced person, on the other hand, is totally uninvolved personally and unable to appreciate what he or she perceives because "it wasn't done right" or "the sermon should have been written another way." The balance suggested here is to minimize distance without losing it altogether. See Friedman, "Theater and Therapy," 3.

10. Emotional objectivity has to do with the ability to be neutral about the emotional process. Neutrality is best fostered from a system perspective where one is aware of as many variables as possible in the emotional field. The awareness of the many variables helps one to be neutral about what is occurring in the field. See discussion of neutrality in Michael E. Kerr and Murray Bowen, *Family Evaluation* (New York: W. W. Norton, 1988), 111, 254–55.

11. Jay E. Adams, *Preaching with Purpose* (Grand Rapids: Zondervan, 1982), 86.

12. Ibid., 86.

13. Ibid., 97–103.

14. Ibid., 97.

15. Also see Thomas H. Troeger, *Imagining a Sermon* (Nashville: Abingdon, 1990); Patricia Wilson-Kastner, *Imagery for Preaching* (Minneapolis: Fortress Press, 1989).

16. Adams lists as an example Charles Spurgeon, and refers to his own book, *Sense Appeal in the Sermons of Charles Haddon Spurgeon* (Phillipsburg, N.J.: Presbyterian and Reformed Publishing Co., 1975).

17. Walter Wink, *Unmasking the Powers* (Philadelphia: Fortress Press, 1986), 25.

18. Job disdains the justifications his friends Eliphaz, Bildad, Zophar, and the young theological student, Elihu, provide for his suffering, beginning in Job 3, and is comforted by God's appearance in chapter 40.

19. Keith D. Miller, *Voice of Deliverance: The Language of Martin Luther King Jr. and Its Sources* (New York: Free Press, 1992), 20.

20. Both James A. Forbes Jr. and Gardner C. Taylor have works listed in the bibliography.

21. For more discussion of these forms see James Earl Massey, *Designing the Sermon* (Nashville: Abingdon, 1980), 20–24.

22. Mitchell, *Celebration and Experience in Preaching*, 37–47.

4. DESIGNING FOR CELEBRATION

1. Friedman, "Theater and Therapy," 9.

2. Edwin H. Friedman in oral presentation at the Center for Family Process (Bethesda, Md.), January 1994.

3. I believe one of the most insidious traps of congregational life is when the clergyperson ends up with the responsibility for the lives and salvation of the members, and the church itself. This overfunctioning position is absolutely lethal to the health, well-being, and spiritual life of the pastor and the congregation.

4. This does not mean that the preacher must always provide definitive answers and certainty. "I am not sure" or "I do not know" can be a valid stance and position for God's spokesperson.

5. I heard James A. Forbes Jr. instruct preaching students not to purchase one book of sermons or sermon illustrations to look for material until they consulted the "archives of their own soul." Superbly effective stories or illustrations occur in preaching only if the preacher consults the archives of his/her intuitive soul.

6. Viktor E. Frankl, *From Death-Camp to Existentialism*, trans. Ilse Lasch (Boston: Beacon Hill Press, 1959), xi.

7. This corresponds to the distinction between exegesis and hermeneutics in Krister Stendahl, *Paul among Jews and Gentiles* (Philadelphia: Fortress Press, 1976), 35–36. Stendahl believes exegesis aims at discovering what the text *meant* to its first readers; hermeneutics tries to ascertain what the text might mean to readers today.

8. Admittedly, it was easier for me to believe, since I was not the one dying of cancer, but the preacher must believe the text to authentically minister/preach the text. To truly minister/preach *in* the name of Jesus, one must be *of* the name of Jesus. One cannot effectively preach to life and death concern what one does not deeply believe.

9. We need a homiletic method that helps look at the preacher's core belief. What intuitive tapes are running in the preacher influencing the discovery of meaning in the text? Will the preacher allow the text to over-

record or strengthen his or her intuitive tapes in core belief? Will the preacher encounter the text in the way the preacher asks the people to encounter it?

10. W. B. Stevens, arranged by J. R. Baxter Jr., "Farther Along," *New National Baptist Hymnal* (Nashville: National Baptist Publishing Board, 1983), 326.

11. The sermon is entitled "Where Are the Smiths?" The full Preaching Worksheet and sermon text are included in chapter 6.

12. Jay E. Adams, *Truth Applied* (Grand Rapids: Zondervan Publishing House, 1990), 33–34 (emphasis added).

13. Davis, *Design for Preaching,* 37.

14. Wyatt T. Walker, *The Soul of Black Worship* (New York: Martin Luther King Fellows Press, 1984), 17.

15. Of course, much more needs to be said about this critical aspect of sermon preparation; see Davis, *Design for Preaching*, 202–20, 265–94.

16. "Lift Every Voice and Sing," *New National Baptist Hymnal,* 477.

17. James Weldon Johnson, *Along This Way* (New York: Da Capo Press, 1973), 154–56.

18. Kenneth Atchity, *A Writer's Time: A Guide to the Creative Process, from Vision through Revision* (New York: W. W. Norton, 1986).

5. GUIDELINES FOR CELEBRATION

1. Mitchell starts to define and give method for celebration in his first work, *Black Preaching,* 188–95; he further expands his thought to a full chapter on celebration in his second work, *The Recovery of Preaching,* 53–73; and in his next preaching text, it becomes so central to his homiletic method that he includes it as part of the title, *Celebration and Experience in Preaching* (see pages 61–76). It is from the first book that the term "ecstatic reinforcement" is drawn.

2. Mitchell, *Celebration and Experience in Preaching,* 34.

3. T. S. Eliot, *The Complete Poems and Plays 1909–1950* (New York: Harcourt Brace Jovanovich, 1962), 145.

4. Linda Villarosa, "Revelations," *Essence* 26, no. 5 (September 1995): 92.

5. I believe it is not necessarily what one believes, or the position one takes based upon what one believes, that is the critical matter in relationships with people. The critical matter is how one functions with what one believes, and how one functions with the position one takes. Regardless of one's position or belief, certain kinds of functioning, such as condemning people to hell, are negative and detrimental. It is more important to look at how people function than to judge them on the basis of the values they express.

6. Again, I do not know many preachers who would not unequivocally state that they believe in the healing, forgiving, and loving power of the gospel. I am not questioning what we say we believe, but how we function with what we believe. How we function with what we believe has to do with the question of maturity, and what resides in the preacher's core belief. When we move in the arena of "righteous indignation," we must be careful to discern biblical from personal offense. We need a homiletical method that helps to discern the preacher's core belief and the preacher's maturity.

7. Some suggest that "fire and brimstone" preaching with its guilt and fear is the best way to motivate people for Christ. Some attempt to "dangle sinners over the fires of hell until the heat singes their flesh and garments." Would that we could be as sense descriptive about God's love and salvation as these preachers are about hell and damnation. I believe there is no better motivation for people to come to God than experiential invitation to the healing and forgiving love of God.

8. Hallie, *Lest Innocent Blood Be Shed*, 24.

9. Martin Luther, "A Mighty Fortress Is Our God," trans. Fredrick H. Hedge, *New National Baptist Hymnal*, 22.

10. John Lovell Jr., *Black Song: The Forge and the Flame* (New York: Paragon House, 1986), cover notes.

11. "Oh, What a Beautiful City," traditional Negro spiritual, located in *Songs of Zion* (Nashville: Abingdon, 1981), 169.

12. Kathleen Battle and Jessye Norman, *The Spirituals*, recorded live at Carnegie Hall, New York, 18 March 1990 (Hamburg: Deutsche Grammophon, 1991).

13. For the Lord himself, with a cry of command, with the archangel's call and with the sound of God's trumpet, will descend from heaven, and the dead in Christ will rise first. Then we who are alive, who are left, will be caught up in the clouds together with them to meet the Lord in the air; and so we will be with the Lord forever.

14. Dottie Rambo, "We Shall Behold Him," *Gospel: One Hundred Songs of Devotion*, The Ultimate Series (Milwaukee: Hal Leonard Publishing Corp.), 258–61.

15. For serious study of one of the classic whoopers in the African American tradition, C. L. (Clarence LaVaughn) Franklin, see C. L. Franklin, *Give Me This Mountain: Life History and Selected Sermons*, ed. Jeff Todd Titon (Chicago: University of Illinois Press, 1989).

16. See Mitchell, "A History of Black Preaching," in *Black Preaching,* esp. 28–34.

6. THREE SERMONS ILLUSTRATING METHOD

1. This sermon in seed form was a gift to me from Dr. John Lavender, former pastor of First Baptist Church of Bakersfield, California, upon his retirement from pastoral ministry.

2. Eliza E. Hewitt and Emily D. Wilson, "When We All Get to Heaven," *New National Baptist Hymnal,* 429.

3. David F. Payne, *First and Second Samuel,* Daily Bible Study Series (Philadelphia: Westminster Press, 1982), 68.

4. "Naaman" written by Eleanor Wright (Brentwood, Tenn.: Songs of Promise/BMI/EMI Christian Music Publishing).

Selected Bibliography

Adams, Jay E. *Preaching with Purpose*. Grand Rapids: Zondervan Publishing House, 1986.

―――. *Sense Appeal in the Sermons of Charles Haddon Spurgeon*. Phillipsburg, N.J.: Presbyterian and Reformed Publishing Co., 1975.

――― *Truth Applied*. Grand Rapids: Zondervan Publishing House, 1990.

Armstrong, Richard H. "Reversals: Their Care and Feeding." *Georgetown Family Symposia* 1 (1971–1972): 139.

Atchity, Kenneth. *A Writer's Time: A Guide to the Creative Process, from Vision through Revision*. New York: W. W. Norton, 1986.

Blackwood, Andrew W. *The Fine Art of Preaching*. New York: Macmillan, 1937.

Bowen, Murray. *Family Therapy in Clinical Practice*. Northvale, N.J.: Jason Aronson, 1990.

Bowyer, Richard O., Betty L. Hart, and Charlotte A. Meade. *Prayer in the Black Tradition*. Nashville: Upper Room Press, 1987.

Broadus, John A. *On the Preparation and Delivery of Sermons*. 4th ed. rev. by Vernon L. Stanfield. San Francisco: Harper & Row, 1979.

Buttrick, David. *Homiletic: Moves and Structures*. Philadelphia: Fortress Press, 1987.

Crum, Milton. *Manual on Preaching: A New Process of Sermon Design*. Valley Forge, Pa.: Judson Press, 1977.

Crawford, Evans E., with Thomas H. Troeger. *The Hum: Call and Response in African American Preaching*. Nashville: Abingdon Press, 1995.

Davis, H. Grady. *Design for Preaching*. Philadelphia: Fortress Press, 1985.

DeForest, Cathy. "The Art of Conscious Celebration: A New Concept for Today's Leaders." In *Transforming Leadership: From Vision to Results*. Edited by John D. Adams. Alexandria: Miles River Press, 1986.

Dunn, James. "Models of Christian Community in the New Testament." In *The Church Is Charismatic.* Edited by Arnold Bittlinger. Geneva: World Council of Churches, 1981.

Eliot, T. S. *The Complete Poems and Plays 1909–1950.* New York: Harcourt Brace Jovanovich, 1962.

Fenner, Thomas P. *Religious Folk Songs of the Negro.* Hampton, Va.: The Institute Press, 1909.

Forbes, James A., Jr. *The Holy Spirit and Preaching.* Nashville: Abingdon Press, 1989.

Frankl, Viktor E. *Psychotherapy and Existentialism: Selected Papers on Logotherapy.* New York: Simon & Schuster, 1967.

Franklin, C. L. *Give Me This Mountain: Life History and Selected Sermons.* Edited by Jeff Todd Titon. Chicago: University of Illinois Press, 1989.

Friedman, Edwin H. "Bowen Theory and Therapy." In *Handbook of Family Therapy.* Vol. 2. Edited by Alan S. Gurman and David P. Kniskern. New York: Brunner/Mazel, 1991.

———. *Generation to Generation: Family Process in Church and Synagogue.* New York: Guilford Press, 1985.

——— "Theater and Therapy." *The Family Therapy Networker* 8, no. 1 (January–February 1984): 2.

Gospel: 100 Songs of Devotion, The Ultimate Series. Milwaukee: Hal Leonard Publishing Corp., 258–61.

Hallie, Philip. *Lest Innocent Blood Be Shed.* New York: Harper & Row, 1979.

Harris, James H. *Preaching Liberation.* Minneapolis: Fortress Press, 1995.

Henry, Matthew. *A Commentary of the Whole Bible.* Reference Library Edition. 6 vols. Old Tappan, N.J.: Fleming H. Revell Company, n.d.

Hobbie, Wellford F. "The Play Is the Thing: New Forms for the Sermon." *Journal for Preachers* 5, no. 4 (1982): 18.

The Holy Bible, New International Version. New York: New York International Bible Society, 1978.

Johnson, James Weldon. *Along This Way.* New York: Da Capo Press, 1973.

Kaiser, Otto. *The Books of the Prophet Isaiah,* 2d ed. 3 vols., *Isaiah 1–12, Isaiah 13–39, Isaiah 40–66.* Translated by John Bowden. Philadelphia: Westminster Press, 1983.

Kerr, Michael E., and Murray Bowen. *Family Evaluation.* New York: W. W. Norton, 1988.

King, Martin Luther, Jr. "I've Been to the Mountaintop," 3 April 1968, Memphis. In James W. Washington, *A Testament of Hope: The Essential Writings of Martin Luther King Jr.* San Francisco: Harper & Row, 1986.

Koenig, John. *Charismata: God's Gifts for God's People.* Philadelphia: Westminster Press, 1978.

Lischer, Richard. *The Preacher King.* New York: Oxford University Press, 1995.

Lovell, John, Jr. *Black Song: The Forge and the Flame.* New York: Paragon House, 1986.

Lowry, Eugene. *The Homiletical Plot: The Sermon as Narrative Art Form.* Atlanta: John Knox Press, 1980.

————. *How to Preach a Parable.* Nashville: Abingdon Press, 1989.

Martin, Ralph. *The Spirit and the Congregation: Studies in 1 Corinthians 12–15.* Grand Rapids: Eerdmans Publishing Co., 1984.

Massey, James Earl. *Designing the Sermon.* Nashville: Abingdon Press, 1980.

Miller, Keith D. *Voice of Deliverance: The Language of Martin Luther King Jr. and Its Sources.* New York: Free Press, 1992.

Mitchell, Henry H. *Black Preaching.* Philadelphia: J. B. Lippincott, 1970. Reprint: San Francisco: Harper & Row, 1979.

————. *Black Preaching: The Recovery of a Powerful Art.* Nashville: Abingdon Press, 1990.

————. *Celebration and Experience in Preaching.* Nashville: Abingdon Press, 1990.

————. *The Recovery of Preaching.* San Francisco: Harper & Row, 1977.

The New National Baptist Hymnal, Nashville: National Baptist Publishing Board, 1983.

Payne, David F. *First and Second Samuel.* The Daily Bible Study Series. Philadelphia: Westminster Press, 1982.

Proctor, Samuel D. *The Certain Sound of the Trumpet: Crafting a Sermon of Authority.* Valley Forge, Pa.: Judson Press, 1994.

Scarboro, Glenn N. "The Delusions of Differentiation: Notations on Family Process." In *The Therapist's Own Family,* edited by Peter Titelman, 81. Northvale, N.J.: Jason Aronson, 1992.

The Song Goes On. Chicago: Covenant Publications, 1990.

Stendahl, Krister. *Paul among Jews and Gentiles.* Philadelphia: Fortress Press, 1976.

Spielberg, Steven. *The Color Purple.* Burbank: Warner Home Video, 1987. Film.

Taylor, Barbara Brown. *The Preaching Life.* Cambridge, Mass.: Cowley Publications, 1993.

Taylor, Gardner C. *How Shall They Preach.* Elgin, Ill.: Progressive Publishing House, 1977.

Troeger, Thomas H. *Imagining a Sermon*. Nashville: Abingdon Press, 1990.

Vaughan, Curtis. "Colossians." In *The Expositor's Bible Commentary*. General Editor, Frank E. Gaebelein. Grand Rapids: Regency Reference Library, Zondervan Publishing House, 1978.

Walker, Alice. *The Color Purple*. New York: Washington Square Press, 1982.

Walker, Wyatt T. *Somebody's Calling My Name*. Valley Forge, Pa.: Judson Press, 1979.

———. *The Soul of Black Worship*. New York: Martin Luther King Fellows Press, 1984.

Wilder, Amos N. *Early Christian Rhetoric: The Language of the Gospel*. New York: Harper & Row, 1964.

Wilson-Kastner, Patricia. *Imagery for Preaching*. Minneapolis: Fortress Press, 1989.

Wink, Walter. *Naming the Powers*. Vol. 1. *The Powers*. Philadelphia: Fortress Press, 1984.